TRUE WEREWOLVES
OF HISTORY

TRUE WEREWOLVES
OF HISTORY

by
DONALD F. GLUT

SENSE OF WONDER PRESS
James A. Rock & Company, Publishers
Rockville • Maryland

TRUE WEREWOLVES OF HISTORY
by Donald F. Glut

SENSE OF WONDER PRESS
is an imprint of JAMES A. ROCK & CO., PUBLISHERS

Front Cover Art: After a detail from a stained glass window, Notre Dame de Paris.

Back Cover: 15th Century woodcut of "werewolf in battle."

Frontispiece: An early woodcut of a werewolf baying at the moon.

Address comments and inquiries to: SENSE OF WONDER PRESS
James A. Rock & Company, Publishers
9710 Traville Gateway Drive, #305
Rockville, MD 20850

E-mail:
jrock@rockpublishing.com   lrock@senseofwonderpress.com
Internet URL: www.SenseOfWonderPress.com

Paperbound ISBN: 0-918736-69-2
Hardbound ISBN: 0-918736-70-6

Printed in the United States of America

First Edition: December 2004

To WILLIAM DONALD GROLLMAN,
Who would have preferred a how-to-do-it book.

Contents

AUTHOR'S INTRODUCTION
True Vampires of History

I'd never been a believer in "werewolves", until my aunt's sister-in-law related a case of apparent lycanthropy on record in a prominent Chicago hospital.

During World War II, the hospital in which the woman was a Red Cross worker had a rather distinguished guest. He was a sturdy black man confined for no apparent reason. He was in the best physical health and possessed a most pleasing personality—that is, until the full moon rose. During the cycle of the full moon he had to be locked in a room where he would proceed to howl like a wolf and rip the furnishings to shreds. Had he encountered anyone during those lapses, in which he believed himself to be a wolf, he may have satisfied his craving for human blood by ripping into their throats with his teeth.

This was the first instance of actual lycanthropy I had ever encountered.

In the strict and "classic" sense, the inmate of that hospital was not a true werewolf. He did not actually transform into an animal or a hybrid of man and beast. But from his own viewpoint he apparently did transform, his hands metamorphosing into shaggy claws, his teeth enlarging into sharp fangs that begged to sever a human jugular vein. He was, rather, a lycanthrope, a man whose belief that he changed into a beast was such that he *acted* the role of that beast. Indeed, the victim of a lycanthrope would be little better off than the victim of a werewolf.

Generally, in this book, the term "lycanthrope" refers to those unfortunates who believe themselves to be transformed into beasts without undergoing an actual physical metamorphosis. "Werewolf" mostly pertains to those physically changed into animals or hybrids. These include such werewolves as the woman of Saintonge who, while in wolf form, caught her paw in a trap and wore a glove to hide the mutilation for the rest of her life; the two warlocks executed at Liege in 1810 for transforming into wolves and devouring several children, tossing the uneaten portions to their twelve-year-old colleague, who took on the form of a raven; and the *loup-garau* that plagued a field near Champigni, France, during the night of 1863, as reported by Reverend Sabine Baring-Gould in *The Book of Were-Wolves: Being an Account of a Terrible Superstition* (1865).

As with my earlier book *True Vampires of History*, I have not attempted to trace the origins of werewolfery or investigate the truths behind the beliefs in werewolves or other were-creatures. I present here a collection of cases of werewolfery and lycanthropy (including some cases of men supposedly transformed into tigers, leopards, jaguars, and so forth, and omitting the countless instances of witches changing themselves into cats and hares). For in-depth reading on the subject, I refer you to the bibliography, especially, recommending *The Werewolf*, by Montague Summers, *Werwolves*, by Elliott O'Donnell, and for an investigation of other species of were-animal, *The Terror of the Leopard Men*, by Juba Kennerley.

All cases in this book are "true" or were at least *believed* to be true when first recorded. Oftentimes, legend and fact run together, making it difficult to differentiate between them. I make no judgements since I was fortunately not present at any of the cited incidents. Perhaps you, in reading each case, will deduce some misinterpretation by those involved in the accounts. Like the grim-faced men who resided over the werewolf trials of the Middle Ages, with the power to send a defendant to the stake, you must be the judge.

If you are expecting the romantic werewolf of myriad motion pictures, characterized by Lon Chaney, Jr.'s Wolf Man, to haunt these pages, you are in for a disapointment, perhaps a shock, at least a surprise. The Werewolf that sends peasants cowering behind locked doors is not necessarily the same handsome young man who does little more than sprout neatly trimmed fur and prowl through the moonlit moors in search of a jugular vein, which (at least in the older films) he frequently bites tastefully in the shadows. The werewolves and other were-animals in this book are usually less refined, liking nothing better than eating the flesh of their victims and leaving the scattered remains of corpses about for a later snack.

For those of you who contemplate the unknown or who believe that there might be things in this universe beyond the philosophy of Horatio — and who can endure the grisly accounts of human monstrosities performing the most degrading acts — welcome to the world of the werewolf. And think twice the next time you cross a moonlit field and hear a bush rustling in the breeze, the howl of a distant dog — or a wolf.

—Donald F. Glut

WEREWOLVES OF ARCADIA

In the Eighth Book of *Description of Greece* (Second Century), Pausanias described the werewolves of Arcadia:

"The Arcadians say that Pelasgus was the first man who lived in this land ... Pelasgus' son Lycaon outdid his father in the ingenuity of the schemes he projected. For he built a city Lycosura in Mount Lycaeugs, he gave to Zeus the surname of Supreme, and he refused to sacrifice anything that had life ... Whereas Lycaon brought a human babe to the altar of Lycaean Zeus, and sacrificed it, and poured out the blood on the altar; and they say that immediately after the sacrifice he was turned into a wolf. For my own part I believe the tale: it has been handed down among the Arcadians from antiquity, and probability is in its favour .... They say that from the time of Lycaon downwards a man has always been turned into a wolf at the sacrifice of Lycaean Zeus, but that the transformation is not for life; for if, while he is a wolf, he abstains from human flesh, in the ninth year afterwards he changes back into a man, but if he has tasted human flesh he remains a beast for ever."

There have been different versions of this story. Hyginus told of the child Arcas, being born of a union between Zeus and Pelasgo's daughter Callisto, in his *Fabelae*. Both Hyginus in the *Poeticon Astronomicon* and Erastosthenes in the *Castaserimoi* related how Lycaon sacrificed Arcas upon the altar. The enraged Zeus turned Lycaon into a wolf and blasted his sons with bolts of lightning.

Lycophron stated that there was more than one werewolf involved in his *Alexandre*. According to Lycophron, the flesh of Nuktimos, Lycaon's youngest child, was boiled in the sacrifice. But Zeus became so angry that he changed Lycaon and all of his sons into wolves.

Jupiter's first person account of the tale was set down by Ovid in book I of his *Metamorposes* (translated by Jon Dryden in 1693):

> The Clamours of this vile degenerate Age,
> The Cries of Orphans, and th' Oppressor's Rage
> Had reach'd the Stars; I will descend, said I,
> In hope to prove this loud Complaint a Lye.

Disguise'd in Humane Shape, I Travell'd round
The World, and more than what I hear'd, I found.
O're *Maenalus* I took my steepy way,
By Caverns infamous for Beasts of Prey:

Then cross'd *Cyllene,* and the piny shade
More infamous, by Curst *Lycaon* Made.
Dark Night had cover'd Heav'n and Earth, Before
I enter'd his Unhospitable Door.
Just at my entrance, I display'd the Sign
That somewhat was approaching of Divine.
The prostrate People pray; the Tyrant grins;
And, adding Prophanation to his Sins,
I'll try, said he, and if a God appear
To prove his Deity, shall cost him dear.
Twas late; the Graceless Wretch, my Death prepares,
When I shou'd soundly Sleep, opprest with Cares;
This dire Experiment, he chose, to prove
If I were Mortal, or undoubted *Jove*:
But first he had a resolv'd to taste my Pow'r
Not long before, but in a luckless hour
Some Legates, sent from the *Molossian* State,
Were on a peaceful Errant come to Treat;
Of these he Murders one, he boils the Flesh;
And lays the mangl'd Morsels in a Dish;
Some part he Roasts; then serves it up, so drest,
And bids me welcome to this Humane Feast.
Mov'd with disdain, the Table I o're-turn'd;
And with avenging Flames, the Place burn'd.
The Tyrant in a fright, for shelter, gains
The Neigb'ring Fields, and scours along the plains.
Howling he fled, and fain he wou'd have spoke;
But Humane Voice, his Brutal Tongue forsook.
About his lips, the gather'd foam he churns,
And, breathing slaughters, still with rage he burns,
But on the bleating Flock, his fury turns.
His Mantel, now his Hide, with rugged hairs
Cleaves to his back, a famish'd face he bears.
His arms descend, his shoulders sink away,

To multiply his legs for chace of Prey.
He grows a Wolf, his hoariness remains,
His eyes still sparkle in a narr'wer space;
His jaws retain the grin, and violence of face.

In *The Werewolf*, Montague Summers held as more valuable the following version by Pliny in book viii, chapter xxii of his *Naturrall Historie* (translated by Philemon Holland in 1601).

"That men may be transformed into wolves, and restored againe to their former shape, we must confidently believe to be a lowd lie, or else give credit to all those tales which wee have for so many ages found to be meere fabulous untruths. But how this opinion grew first, and is come to be so firmly setled, that when wee would give men the most opprobrious words of defiance that we can, wee tearme them *Versipelles* (i.e. Turncoats), I thinke it not much amisse in a word to shew. *Euanthes* (a writer among the Greekes, of good account and authoritie) reporteth, that hee found among the records of the Arcadians, That in Arcadia there was a certain house and race of the *Antaei*, out of which one evermore must of necessitie be transformed into a wolfe: and when they of that family have cast lots who it shall be, they use to accompany the prate upon whom the lot is flange, to certaine meere or poole in that countrey: when he is thither come, they turn him naked out of all his clothes, which they hang upon an oke nearby; then he swimmeth over the said lake to the other side, and being entred into the wildernesse, is presently transfigured and turned into a wolfe, and so keepeth companie with his like of that kind for nine yeeres space: during which time, (if he forbeare all the while to eat mans flesh) he retruneth again to the same poole or pond, and being swomme over it, receiveth his former shape againe of a man, save onely that hee shall looke nine yeeres elder than before. *Fabius* addeth one thing more and saith, That he findeth again the same apparele that was hung up in the oke aforesaid. A wonder it is to see, to what passe these Greekes are come in there is not so shameless a lye, but it findeth one or other of them to uphold and maintaine it. And therefore *Agriopas*, who wrote at OlympionicF, telleth a tale of one *Deemoetus Parrhasius*, That he upon a time at a certain solemne sacrifice (which the Arcadians celebrated in honour of *Iupiter Lycaeus*) tasted of the inwards of a child that was killed for a sacrifice, according to the manner of the Arcadians (which even was to shed mans blood in their devine service) and so was turned into a wolfe: and the same man ten yeeres after became a man againe, was present at the

exercise of the publicke games, wrestled, did his devoir, and went away
with victorie home againe from Olympia. Over and besides, it is commonly thought and verily beleeved, that in the taile of this beast, there
is a little string or haire that is effectuall to procure love, and that when
he is taken at any time, hee casteth it away from him, for that it is of no
force and verture unlesse it be taken from him whiles he is alive. He
goeth to rut in the whole yeere not above twelve daies."

Annual
Neuri Werewolves

Ancient Greece had a variety of werewolf that only changed into
animal form once a year. These werewolves were the Neuri, a mysterious group of nomads who lived around the Bug river basin between
what is now Lithuania and Poland. The Neuri were known sorcerers,
although Herodotus of Halicarnassus (484-404) denied their ability to
shift their shapes in this fourth book *Melpomene.*

"The Neuri have the same customs as the Scythians. In the generation before that land was invaded by Darius the whole nation was forced
to migrate on account of the plague of serpents, since not only did
their own territory produce very many, but even vaster numbers thrust
in on them from the deserts of the north. Being thus tormented they
abandoned their native soil and took refuge with the Budini. It appears
that the Neuri are sorcerers, and such they are confidently held to be
both by the Scythians and by the Greek settlers in Scythie, who related
that once every year each Naurian becomes a wolf for a few days, and
then again resumes his original form. This, however, they will never
pursuade me to believe, although they assert it roundly and confirm
their statement by a solemn oath."

According to Pomponius Mela in his *De Situ Orbis, Of the Situation
of the World*: (translated by Arthur Golding in *The Rare and Singular
worke of Pomponius Mela,* 1590):

"The Neures haue a certaine time to euerie of them limitted, wherein
they may (if they will) be chaunged into Woolves, and returne to their
former shape againe."

Solonius adds:

"The Neuri indeed, as we are told, at certain seasons are transformed
into wolves, and then after a given time, assigned by lot, they recover
their original form."

St. Ronan

St. Ronan died in 540 but not before being accused of transforming into a wolf to satisfy some very unsaintly cravings. Born in Ireland, Ronan had settled in Brittany in the year 510. There he preached Christianity and became despised by many people whose beliefs were contrary to his own.

An old woman named Keban took a particular disliking to Ronan. The complaint she made to King Grallon was enough to have Ronan put to death.

According to the woman, Ronan was a werewolf who roamed through the countryside, attacking sheep and cattle, and that he had sunk his fangs into her son and then devoured him.

Luckily Ronan was able to disprove the woman's accusations and forgave her slanderous speech.

Were-Bear vs. Were-Bear

Rerir was an ugly, hunchbacked berserker of Iceland, who dearly loved Signi, the lovely daughter of a neighboring berserker. When she scorned the love of the misshapen man he retaliated with a plan of vengeance.

Rerir was both a werewolf and a were-bear. Since the bear was the more powerful of the two animals, he assumed that shape and climbed the onto Signi's roof. He ripped the roof apart with incredible strength, then dropped into the house on his grim mission.

A servant was the first to encounter the monster and was crushed in the shaggy arms of the were-bear. The beast silently entered the room of Signi's parents, smashing in her mother's skull with a single sweep of his paw.

Unknown to Rerir, however, was the fact that Signi's father was also a were-bear. He made the transformation and immediately lunged for his Rerir. The house virtually shook as the two monsters endeavored to destroy one another. Signi, hearing the sounds of the battle, rushed into the room hoping to save her father. But, as she struck with her knife, she accidentally stabbed the wrong bear to death.

The cook provided the final solution for eliminating the were-bear. She mixed a concoction of sulpher, castoreum and asafoetida and then hurled it into the beast's face. Instantly, the monster's visage metamorphosed into the familiar and unpleasant face of Rerir.

The hunchback was now at the mercy of the remaining family and the servants. Signi ordered that Rerir be bound and given a short trial in the morning, after which he was promptly executed.

Prince Balanus

In the year 970, Peter and Balanus, the sons of King Simeon, ruled Bulgaria.

Balanus was slightly different from his brother, for he was more than a mere prince. He had made a pact with Satan in return for numerous powers, making him the greatest magician of his day.

Among the abilities that he acquired from the Devil was shapeshifting. Baianus would delight in transforming himself into wolf or any other beast of his fancy. He was an evil sort and his ability to change into a wolf often proved an aid to him. After all, there were many things a wolf could do that a prince could not.

The history of Prince Balanus is related by Joannes Tritheim, Abbot or Sponheim, in his *Annales Hirsaugienses.*

POPE LEO
AND THE WITCHES

A certain pair of witches in the Eleventh Century prospered by magically transforming men into various animals and then selling them. The witches ran an inn on one of the main roads leading to Rome. Here they would drink and carry on, all the while awaiting a new patron to their establishment who might add to their purses by being sold as an animal.

In one instance, the two witches worked their shape-changing powers on a young man, who later reported to Pope Leo IX during the early part of his reign (which began on February 12,1049). The story was recorded by many scholars, including Baptista Fulgosi in his *Dicta Factaque Memorabilia* (1509), Jeans Bodin's *Demonomanie* (1580), and Henri Boguet's *Discours des Sorciers* (1590).

The young man, who was unfortunate enough to visit the witches' inn, was turned into an ass. Although he had an animal's body, his mind was still that of a man. Therefore the ass was easily able to obey the commands of the witches when they exhibited the beast. The animal was indeed marvelous and capable of performing many difficult tricks.

The inn was soon crowded with people who had come long distances to see the remarkable ass. Among the patrons was a rich nobleman who thought the animal was the perfect addition to his personal collection. He paid the witches the price they demanded for the beast and took it away with the understanding that it should never enter the water.

With such a stipulation made by two hags, the nobleman should have suspected that something was amiss. Instead, he gave the beast to the care of his servant, who was careful to keep it out of the water.

The nobleman's banquets and parties were livened by the performances of the wonderful animal with the human mind. Seeing the beast do its tricks delighted the guests as they guzzled down their wine and cheered.

But the human mind of the beast was plotting. One day, when its keeper happened to turn away, the ass escaped and ran into the lake. It was a human being who emerged from the water.

The nobleman was aghast, as the young man told what had happened. Immediately the two hags were taken into custody. After a grueling interrogation, they admitted what they had done to the boy.

Pope Leo did not to believe this story.

There was an investigation, carried on by a priest named Peter Damian. When the investigation was over and the Pontiff reviewed the facts of the case, he no longer doubted that the witches had indeed transformed the young man into an ass.

WEREWOLVES AND ST. PATRICK

Ireland has had its share of werewolves, some caused by the forces of Evil and others by the powers of Good, depending upon the reputation of the one causing the transformation. The Druids engaged in transforming themselves into animals, according to the *Leabhar Na H-Uidhri* or *The Book of the dun Cow,* the oldest of all Irish books (written in approximately 1100).

To be an Irish werewolf, a man did not have to suffer a curse or make a pact with Satan. He could have the singular misfortune of being born into a family who had the affliction in its blood. *The Coir Anmann (Fitness of Names)* stated:

"Laignech *Faelad*. That is, he was the man that used to shift into *fealad*, i.e. wolf-shapes. He and his offspring after him used to go, whenever they pleased, into the shapes of wolves, kill the herds. Wherefore he was called Laignech *Faelad*, for he was the first of them (the group composed of Laignech and his descendants) to go into wolf-shape."

The great St. Patrick was also said to have the ability to transform men into beasts. Naturally, when he did his bits of wizardry, his powers were not attributed to the Devil. In the Norse *Kongs Skuggsjo (Speculum Regele)* Written about 1250, the following was said about the Irish saint:

"There is also in that land one wonderful thing, which will seem very untruthful to men. Yet the people who inhabit that land say that it is certainly true. And that befell on account of the wrath of a holy man. It is said that when the holy Patricus was preaching Christianity in that land, there was one great race more hostile to him than the other people that were in the land. And these men tried to do him many kinds of injury. And when he preached Christianity to them as to other men, and came to meet them when they were holding their assembly, then they took this counsel, to howl at him like wolves. But when he saw that his message would succeed little with these people, then he became very wroth, and prayed God that he might avenge it on them by some judgement, that their descendants might forever remember their disobedience. And great punishment and fit a very wonderful has since befallen their descendants; for it is said that all men who come from that race are always wolves at a certain time, and run into the woods and take food like wolves; and they are worse in this that they have human reason, for all their cunning, and such desire and greed for men as for other creatures. And it is said that some become so every seventh year, and, are men during the interval. And some have it so long that they have seven years at once, and are never so afterwards."

"Seeking the Werewolf" from a 19th Century illustration.

THE GHOSTLY WEREWOLF COUNT

The Abbey of Saint-Riquier was burned to ruins in 1131 by Hugues de Camp-d'Avesnes, the Comte de Saint-Pol. The reason for his actions was to kill his two enemies, the Comte de Beaurain-sur-Canche and he Comte d'Auxi, along with their followers, all of whom were holed up in the abbey.

The Count did not take any human lives into consideration in his attempt to eliminate his enemies. Nearly three thousand people fell victim to that blaze of July 28th. The Abbott, miraculously, managed to flee to Abbeville, while the Count proceeded to ravage the vicinity.

When the Count learned that he was soon to encounter the vengeful Louis-le-Gros, he decided to cease all acts of destruction and beg forgiveness from Pope Innocent II. Seeing that he was not about to be forgiven by the Pontiff, the Count tried to show his repentance by erecting the Abbey or Cercamp and endowing it with great wealth.

Apparently his reparation was not enough to atone for the destruction he had brought upon the land. After the Count died, his ghost was seen to haunt the district he had plagued for centuries. The specter was black, forced to bear heavy chains, and appeared in the shape of a "human" wolf.

THE WEREWOLF'S CLOTHING

Marie de France told of a werewolf who depended upon his own clothing in her *Bisclavart*, written during the reign of King Henry II.

A wealthy lord of Brittany was often observed by his wife to sneak out of the house. He would be gone for three days each week. When he returned to the house, he never provided an explanation for his strange absences.

The woman was extremely curious. After repeatedly asking him to tell where he went, the lord finally confessed that he was a werewolf and prowled through the forest regularly on those three days.

As the lord admitted his condition, he had no knowledge of the fact that his wife had a lover and that she was already plotting against him. Inadvertently, he revealed the means by which she and her lover could marry and enjoy his wealth. The lord explained that his clothing was hidden beneath a certain stone in the ruins of an old building. If he ever failed to recover his clothes, he would be doomed to remain a wolf forever.

The woman waited until her husband was again out on one of his lupine excursions. Then she found his clothes and hid them so that she and her lover could be united.

It was much later that the clothing was discovered and replaced. The lord then returned to his human form and uncovered the plot laid by his wife.

MORE
IRISH WEREWOLVES

A case of werewolfery (dated 1182 or 1183) was related in *Topographica Hibernica* (1188) by Giraldus Cambrensis:

"About three years before the arrival of Prince John in Ireland, it chanced that a certain priest, who was journeying from Ulster towards Meath, was benighted in a woods that lies on the boundaries of Meath. Whilst he, and the young lad his companion, were watching by a fire they and kindled under the leafy branches of a large tree; there came up to them a wolf who immediately addressed them in the following words; 'Do not alarm yourselves and do not be in any way afraid. You need not fear, I say, where there is no reason to fear.' The travelers none the less were thrown in a great damp and were astonied. But the wolf reverently called upon the Name of God. The priest then adjured him, straitly charging him by Almighty God and in the Might of the Most Holy Trinity that he should do them no sort of harm, but rather tell them what sort of creature he was who spake with a human voice. The wolf replied with seemly speech, and said: 'In number we are two, to wit a man and a woman, natives of Ossory, and every seven years on account of the curse laid upon our fold by the blessed Abbot S. Netalis, a brace of us are compelled to throw off the human form and appear in the shape of wolves. At the end of seven years, if perchance these two survive they are able to return again to their homes, reassuming the bodies of men, and another two must needs take their place. Howbeit my wife, who labours with me under this sore visitation, lies not far from hence, grievously sick. Wherefore I beseech you of your good charity to comfort her with the aid of your priestly office.' When he had so said, the wolf led the way to a tree at no great distance, and the priest followed him trembling at the strangeness of the thing. In the hollow of the tree he beheld a wolfen, and she was groaning piteously mingled with sad human sighs. Now when she saw the priest she thanked him very courteously and gave praise to God Who had vouchsafed her such consolation in her hour of utmost need.

"The priest then shrived her and gave her all the last rites of Holy Church so far as the houselling. Most ernestly did she entreat him that she might receive her God, and that he would administer to her the crown and all, the Body of the Lord.

"The priest, however, declared that he was not provided with the holy viaticum, when the man-wolf, who had withdrawn apart for a while, came forward and pointed to the wallet, containing a mass-book and some consecrated Hosts, which, according to the use of his country, the good priest was carrying suspended from his neck under his clothing. The man-wolf entreated him not to deny them any longer the Gift of God, which it was not to be questioned, Divine Providence had sent to them. Moreover to remove all doubt, using his claw as a hand, he drew off the pelt from the head of the wolfen and folded it back even as far down as the naval, whereupon there was plainly to be seen the body of and old woman. Upon this the priest, since she so instantly besought him, urged though it may be more by fear than reasoning, hesitated no longer but gave her Holy Communion, which she received most devoutly from his hands. Immediately after this the man-wolf rolled back the skin again, fitting it to its former place.

"These holy rites have been duly rather than regularly performed, the man-wolf joined their company by the fire they had kindled under the tree and showed himself a human being, not a four-footed beast. In the early morning, at cock-light he led them safely out of the wood, and when he left them to pursue their journey he pointed out to them the best and shortest road, giving them directions for a long way. In taking leave also, he thanked the priest most gratefully and in good set phrase for the surpassing kindness he had shown, promising moreover that if it were God's will he should return home (and already two parts of the period during which he was under the malediction had passed) he would take occasion to give further proofs of his gratitude.

"As they were parting the priest inquired of the man-wolf whether the enemy (the English invader) who had now landed on their shores would continue long to possess the land. The wolf replied: 'On account of the sins of our nation and their enourmous wickedness the anger of

God, falling upon an evil generation, hath delivered them into the hands of their enemies. Therefore so long as this foreign people shall walk in the way of the Lord and keep His commandments, they shall be safe and not to be subdued; but if — and easy is the downward path to iniquity and nature prone to evil- it come to pass that through dwelling among us they turn to our whoredoms, then assuredly will they provoke the wrath of the Lord upon them also.'

"It so happened that about two years later when I was passing through Meath, the Bishop of that dioceses had summoned a synod, and had requested the honourable attendance of the Bishops of neighbouring sees and my Lords the Abbots, in order that they might take counsel together concerning this incident which the priest had related to him. The Bishop, learning that I was travelling to those parts, sent two of his priests to me, asking me if it were possible to attend the synod at which a matter of such grave importance was to be deliberated, and if indeed I could not assist in person, he begged me at least to give them my opinion and judgement in writing. When I heard the whole circumstance in detail from the two priests (although indeed I had been told of it before by many others), inasmuch as I was prevented by many weighty affairs from attending the synod, I was fain amend for my absence by giving my advice in a letter. The Bishop and the full synod so far approved of my counsel, that they followed it forthwith, commanding the priest to travel to Rome, and there to lay the whole thing before the Holy Father, delivering to him letters containing the priest's own account, which was certified by the seals of all the Bishops and Abbots who had been present at the conclave.

"It is not to be disputed, but must be most certainly believed that for our salvation the Divine Nature assumed human nature. Now in the present case we find that at God's bidding in order to manifest His supreme power and righteousness by a very miracle human nature assumed the form of a wolf.

"The point arises: Was this creature man or beast? A rational animal is far above the level of a brute beast. Are we to class in the species man a four-footed animal, whose face is bent to the earth, and who cannot indulge in the visible faculty? Would he who slew this animal be a murderer? We reply that the miracles of God are not to be made the subjects of argument and human disputation, but are to be wondered at in all humility.

"... In our won day also we have seen persons, who deeply skilled in magic arts, turned any substance which was of sufficient quantity into fat porkers as they seemed (but curiously they were always of a reddish hue), and these they sold in the markets. None the less the glamour vanished as soon as they crossed any water and the substance returned to its true material form. However carefully they wee kept, they could not retain their spurious appearance more than three days.

"It is commonly known, and has been bitterly complained of in former days as well as now, that certain foul hags in Wales, as well as in Ireland and Scotland, change themselves into the shape of hares, and under this counterfeit form sucking the teats of cows they secretly rob other persons of their milk.

"We hold then with St. Augustine that neither demons nor sorcerers can either create or essentially change their natures; but those, whom God has created are able by His permission to metamorphize themselves so far as mere outward appearance is concerned, so that they appear to be what truly they are not, and the senses of men beholding them are fascinated and deceived by glamour, so that things are not seen as they really exist, but by some phantom power or magic spell the human vision is deluded and mocked inasmuch as it rests upon unreal and fictitious forms."

WEREWOLF
OF AUVERGNE

Although most everyone today associates the werewolf with the full moon, the English werewolf is the rare species partial to moonlight. Gervase of Tillbury in his *Otia Imperialia* (1210-14) told of this type of werewolf:

"*Of men who were wolves.* It is often debated among the learned whether Nabuchodonosor during the allotted time of his penance was indeed essentially metamorphosed into an ox, since all theologians agree that 'twere easier to transform one shape into another than to create out of nothing. Some authors have written that he acted as an ox, and as a beast ate grass and hay, being an ox in all things his shape excepted. One thing I know that among us it is certain there are men who at certain waxings of the moon are transformed into wolves. In Auvergne —(the facts came under my personal observation)—a part of the diocese of Clermont, a certain great noble, Ponce de Castres, outlawed and exiled Raimbaud de Pointe, a valiant soldier, who had long carried arms. When thus banished and became a wandere on the face of the earth, what time Raimbaud was wandering all alone, as if he had been some wild animal. Making his weary way through trackless and untrodden paths, it happened that one night there fell upon him a damp and sore amaze, and he grew frantic being changed into a wolf under which shape he maurauded his own native village, so that the farmers and franklins in terror abandoned their cottages and manors, leaving them empty and tenantless. This fearsome wolf devoured children, and even older persons were attacked by the beast, which tore their flesh grievously with its keen and savage teeth. At last a certain carpenter was bold enough to attack the aggressor, and with a swift blow of his axe lopped off one of the beast's hind paws, whereupon the werewolf at once resumed human shape. Raimbaud publicly acknowledged that he was right glad thus to lose his foot, since such dismembering had rid him forever of the accursed and damned form. For it is commonly reported and held by grave and worthy doctors that if a werewolf be shorn of one of his members he shall then surely recover his original body.

"In the neighborhood of Chalus, in the diocese of Mende and the department of Ardeche, there lived a man, Calcevayra by name, who was a werewolf. Now he at the plenilune was wont to go apart to a distant spot and there stripping himself mother-naked he would lay all his clothes under some sheltered rock or thornbush. Next, nude as he was, he rolled to and fro in the sand until he rose up in the form of a wolf, raging with a wolf's fierce appetites. With gaping jaws and lolling tongue he rushed violently upon his prey, and he used to explain that wolves always run with open mouths because this helps them to sustain their fleetness of foot. If they close their mouths they cannot easily unclench their teeth, wherefore they are more likely to be captured if by any chance they are pursued."

WEREWOLF BY WITCHCRAFT

Jehan de Saintre was a medieval knight who loved a woman with ideas other than returning his love. She had been a veritable prisoner in her castle tower and wanted the pleasures of absolute freedom enjoyed by a werewolf.

"Hither instantly, the Witch-wife: I want her, I want her. Come, quick!"

Two minutes elapsed.

"What! Is she not here yet?"

When the witch arrived, the woman revealed her ghastly wish.

"Now listen carefully ... . I have a caprice (an irresistible hankering, you understand), a hankering to strangle you, to drown you, or deliver you up to the bishop, who has long been wanting you ... You have one way of escape, and one only — to satisfy another hankering of mine, to change me into a she-wolf. I am so tired of my life. I cannot sit still any longer; I long, at any rate o'nights, to gallop free in the forest. I would be done with submissive fools that wait on me, and dogs that deafen me, and blundering horses that jib and refuse the woodland paths."

"But, dear lady, suppose they caught you?"

" ... Insolent woman! I tell you, shall die the death."

"But surely you know the history of the werewolf woman whose paw was cut off ... I should be so grieved to see such an accident!"

" 'Tis my affair I tell you; and I will listen to no excuses ... come, time presses; I have begun to yelp and howl already ... Oh! the joy of it, to go hunting all alone, by the light of the moon, and all alone to pull down the hind with my strong jaws — yes! And men too, if they come across my path; to bite little tender children, — and women too, women best of all! To make my teeth meet in their flesh! ... How I hate them all ... But none of them as bitterly as you. Never start back, I won't bite you; you move my disgust too sorely, and besides, you have no blood in your veins ... Blood, blood! I must have blood!

She could not be refused. "Nothing easier, my lady. Tonight, at nine o'clock, you shall drink the brew. Then lock yourself up in your chamber. While they think you there, you will be another creature, flying through the woods."

In the morning the woman found herself covered with blood and thoroughly exhausted, as if she had spent the night on a successful hunt. But as the woman returned to the witch who had caused the transformation, she changed her tone.

"Sorceress! Sorceress! What an awful power you possess! I should never have thought as much! But now I am terrified and horror-struck ... Ah! they do well to hate you! 'Twill be a good day when you are burned. I will be your death, when so I please. My peasants this very evening would whet their scythes on you if I said one word of the night's doings ... Away with you, vile, black, ugly wretch."

The Beast of Le Gevaudan.

John Lackland

Often cases of werewolfery are confused with those of vampirism and it is sometimes difficult to distinguish one fiend from the other. Generally, the werewolf is a living person transformed into an animal, while the vampire is a corpse that leaves its grave to perform its evil acts.

The story of King John Lackland of England, who died on October 19, 1216, seems to fit more into the vampire tradition, although at the time the bizarre phenomena happened, everyone attributed it to a werewolf.

King John was a nefarious monarch who was pillaging the eastern countries of England. Even churches fell to his greedy desires and slashing sword. One of the places that he pillaged was the Cistercian abbey of Swineshead, near Bolton, where he managed to eat too many peaches. (Some accounts say that the peaches were poisoned by a monk to avenge the wrongs committed by the evil King.) John, dying of dissentry, was taken to Newark. There he perished and, according to his will, was entombed before the altar of Worcester Cathedral, between the shrines of Saints Oswald and Wulstan.

That was when the real evil nature of John Lackland emerged. Loud shrieks and wolf-like howls were heard issuing from his tomb. The Canons of Worcester declared that there must be an end to the terrible manifestations and ordered the corpse to be disinterred and re-buried in unconsecrated earth.

The deed was finished, and yet still the dead King would not rest in his grave. For even after he had been buried, his fetid corpse was seen prowling about the countryside as a blackened werewolf, snarling and terrifying all that he encountered.

Among the writers who have told this story are Amelie Bosquet in *La Normandie romanesque et marveilleuse* (1845).

The Demon Wolf

A case of what was first believed to be that of werewolfery was detailed by Auvergne, Bishop of Paris, in his Thirteenth Century work *De Universo,* under the sub-heading *Qualiter maligni spiritus uexant, et decipiunt homines.*

A man was possessed by an evil spirit. So powerful was this demon that the pitiful host was driven by it to some hidden place and abandoned for dead.

Shortly afterward, a wolf of especially savage nature tormented the nearby village. All who saw the beast were terrified, fearing that the monster would rip them to shreds with its snapping jaws and sharp claws. Hardly anyone doubted that the wolf was actually the man they knew to be possessed, who had now assumed the form of a werewolf.

When the man appeared in the town, they accused him of being a werewolf. To this he readily admitted, believing that he did transform into an animal.

A religious man came to the village and would not accept the fact that the possessed man was indeed a werewolf. He waited until the man retired to his secret place and the wolf again prowled the streets. Then he took with him a group of villagers to prove that the man was innocent of their terrible accusations.

The demoniac was found to be in a trance. The religious man explained that the man did not metamorphose, but that the evil spirit which possessed him actually left his body to enter that of the wolf.

There was still one thing to be done if his theory were to be absolutely proven. The wolf and the entranced man must appear simultaneously.

The religious man brought the demoniac back to consciousness. Using his own special powers, he summoned the wolf, which approached them howling defiantly. Finally he preformed an exorcism that drove the demon from both the wolf and the man forever.

ROLAND BERTIN

During the reign of Louis XIV, André Bonivon's schooner, the *Bonaventure,* ran ashore one night off an estuary of the Rhone. Bonivon had been raiding the Huguenot settlements on the shores of the Gulf of Lions.

During this thunderstorm, Bonivon was caught in a whirlpool that would have drowned him despite his skills as a swimmer. Someone extended a hand and pulled him from the swirling doom. But as Bonivon stepped upon the land and regained his breath, he discovered that he held not a human hand but a shaggy paw.

While Bonivon prayed for forgiveness for wrongs he committed against the Huguenots, believing this to be a punishment from God, he was forcibly led by his hairy rescuer to a house at the edge of a small town. Finally managing to look at the strange being, he found it to be a werewolf. Bonivon tried to run from the house but tripped over a floor mat. The monstrous wolf creature set him again on his feet and left the room.

The werewolf fed him, and as Bonivon ate he could not help but believe he was being fattened up for the beast's next dinner. Lying on the floor was the mangled corpse of a woman, revealing the nature of the werewolf's last lunch; or so he thought.

The windows were barred and escape was impossible. As he pondered his own demise, Bonivon saw the door open. Expecting only the worst, he saw a man dressed as a Huguenot minister enter the room. The minister identified himself as Roland Bertin, whose wife was slaughtered by Bonivon's men when they raided the village. Bertin himself had been taken, at the command of Bonivon, to be tortured when the ship moved out to sea. What Bonivon and his crew did not know was that the minister was a werewolf, bewitched years before by a hag named Mère Grénier (a last name which Elliott O'Donnell associates with hereditary werewolves). It was this Huguenot who saved Bonivon when the ship went ashore.

Roland Bertin confessed that he was a very mild form of werewolf. Never had he killed anything, from insect to human being. He had no desire to start now, which accounted for his saving the life of André Bonivon.

Moved deeply, Bonivon determined never again to take the life of a Huguenot. When he died many years afterwards, it was as the Huguenots' friend.

THE FRENCHMAN AND THE DEVIL

A typical case of werewolfery was recorded in France in 1521.

A Frenchman claimed to have the ability to transform himself into a wolf. This he was able to do between the hours of dusk and dawn. He enjoyed his wolf form, for it gave him total freedom, allowing him to perform his vile deeds without threats to his human self.

While in the shape of a wolf, he delighted in killing and mauling human beings. He also found great satisfaction in having sexual intercourse — not with human women, but with female wolves.

When asked how he was able to accomplish the transformation, the Frenchman replied that he had attended a witches' Sabbath and made a pact with Satan. His reward for making the pact was the ability to change into a wolf by rubbing himself with a special ointment.

WEREWOLVES OF THE CHATEAU

There have always been young men who have delighted in investigating old buildings said to be haunted. A particular chateau near Poitiers, France, was said to have been the haunt of a group of devils and witches.

One Friday, at midnight, about the year 1530, three young men decided to learn the truth behind the rumors concerning the chateau. None of them really believed the stories they had heard and so boldly ventured to the building. They learned that the stories were true when they peeked inside and saw the rites of the sabbat in full progress.

Mutually agreeing that they would be better off in some other location, the three men prepared to sneak away from the chateau. But their spying had not gone unnoticed. Three enormous wolves suddenly emerged from the shadows and charged at them. After considerable fighting, the men escaped the fangs and claws of the wolves, but not before one of them sliced off the ear of a wolf with his sword.

In the morning, the wielder of the sword learned that a known witch of the area was bedridden as the result of her ear being cut off the previous night.

WEREWOLVES ACCORDING TO GOULART AND FINCEL

"Guillaume de Brabant, in the narrative of Wier, repeated by Goulart, has written in his *History* that a certain man of sense and settled understanding was still so tormented by the evil spirit that at a particular season of the year he would think himself a ravening wolf, and would run here and there in the woods, caves, and deserts, chasing little children. It was said that this man was often found running about in the deserts like a man out of his senses and that at last by the grace of God he came to himself and was healed. There was also, as is related by Job Fincel in the second book *On Miracles,* a villager near Paule in the year 1541, who believed himself to be a wolf, and assaulted several men in the fields, even killing some. Taken at last, but not without great difficulty, he stoutly affirmed that he was a wolf, and that the only way in which he differed from other wolves was that they wore their hairy coats on the outside, while he wore his between his skin and his flesh.

Certain persons, more inhuman and wolfish than he, wished to test the truth of this story, and gashed his arms and legs severely. Then learning their mistake and the innocence of the melancholiac, they passed him over to the consideration of the surgeons, in whose hands he died some days after. Those afflicted with this disease are pale, with dark and haggered eyes, seeing only with great difficulty; the tongue is dry, and they suffer very thirsty. Plane and others write that the brain of a bear excites such bestial imaginations. It is even said that one was given to a Spanish gentleman to eat in our times, which so disturbed his mind, that imagining himself to be transformed into a bear, he fled to the mountains and deserts."

Goulart wrote:

"As for the lycanthropes whose imagination was so damaged that by some satanic efficacy they appeared wolves and not men to those who saw them running about and doing all manner of harm, Bodin maintains that the devil can change the shape of one body into that of another, in the great power that God gives him in this elementary world. He says, then, that there may be lycanthropes who really have been transformed into wolves, quoting various examples and histories to prove his contention. In short, after many disputes, he believes in Colt's forms of lycanthropy. And as for the latter, there is represented at the end of this chapter the summary of his proposition, to wit, that men are sometimes transformed into beasts, retaining in that form the human reason: it may be that this comes about by the direct power of God, or it may be that he gives this power to Satan, who carries out his will, or rather his redoubtable judgements. And if we confess (he says) the truths of the sacred history of Daniel, concerning the transformation of Nebuchadnezzar, and the history of Lot's wife changed into motionless stone, changing men into an ox or a stone is certainly possible; and consequently the transformation to other animals as well."

Jean Bodin concluded:

"Job Fincel, in the eleventh book of his *Marvels,* wrote that there was at Padua a lycanthrope who was caught at his wolf-claws cut, and at the same instant he found his arms and feet cut. That is give to strengthen the case against the sorcerers of Vernon (1556) who assembled themselves in an old and ruined chateau under the shape of an infinite number of cats. There happened to arrive there one evening four or five men, who decided to spend the night in the place. They were awakened by a multitude of cats, who assaulted them, killed one of their number, and wounded others. The men, however, succeeded in wounding several of the cats, who found on recovering their human shape that they were badly hurt. And incredible as it may seem, the trial did not proceed.

"... But the five inquisitors who had experimented in these causes have left it in writing that there were three sorcerers in Strasbourge who, in the guise of three large cats, assaulted a labourer, and in defending himself he wounded and dispersed the cats, who found themselves, at the same moment, laid on sick-beds, in the form of woman severely wounded. At the trial they accused him who had struck them, and he told the judges the hour and the place where he had been assaulted by the cats, and how he had wounded them.

WEREWOLVES AT CHRISTMAS

Gaspar Peucer wrote in his *Commentarius De Praecipius Diuinationum Generibus* (1553):

"As for me I had formerly regarded as ridiculous and fabulous the stories I had often heard concerning the transformation of men into wolves; but I have learnt from reliable sources, and from the testimony of reliable witnesses, that such things are not at all doubtful or incredible, since they tell of such transformations taking place twelve days after Christmas in Livonia and the adjacent countries; as they have been proved to be true by the confessions of those who have been proved to be true by the confessions of those who have been imprisoned and tortured for such crimes. Here is the manner in which it is done. Immediately after Christmas day is past, a lame boy goes around calling these slaves of the devil, of which there are a great number, and enjoining them to follow him. If they procrastinate or go too slowly, there immediately appears a tall man with a whip whose thongs are made of iron chains, with which he urges them onwards, and sometimes lashes the poor wretches so cruelly, that the marks of the whips remain on their bodies till long afterwards, and cause them the greatest pain. As soon as they have set out on their road, they are all changed into wolves.

"... They travel in thousands, having for their conductor the bearer of the whip, after whom they march. When they reach the fields, they rush upon the cattle they find there, tearing and carrying away all they

can, and doing much other damage; but they are not permitted to touch
or wound persons. When they approach any rivers, their guide sepa-
rates the waters with his whip, so that they seem to open up and leave a
dry space by which to cross. At the end of twelve days the whole band
scatters, and everyone returns to his home, having regained his own
proper form. This transformation, they say, comes about in this wise.
Those who are changed fall suddenly to the ground as if seized with
epilepsy, and there they lie without life or motion. Their actual bodies
do not move from the spot where they fallen, nor do their limbs turn
to the hairy limbs of a wolf, but the soul or spirit by some fascination
quits the inert body and enters the *spectrum* of a wolf, and when they
have glutted their foul lupine lusts and cravings, by the Devil's power,
the soul re-enters the former human body, whose members are then
energized by the return of life"

WEREWOLVES ACCORDING TO MAGNUS

The last three chapters of the Eighteenth Book of Olaus Magnus'
Historia de Gentibus Septeatrionalibus (1555) concern werewolves.

"In the Feast of Christs Nativity, in the night, at a certain place,
that they are resolved upon themselves, there is gathered together such
a huge multitude of wolves changed from men that dwell in divers
places, which afterwards the same night doth so rage with wonderfull
fiercenesse, both against mankind and other creatures, that are not fierce
by nature, that the Inhabitants of that Country suffer more hurt from
them, than every they do from true naturall Wolves. For as it is proved
they set upon the houses of men that are in the Woods with wonderful
fierceness, and labour to break down the doors, whereby they may destroy both men and other creatures that remain there. They go into
Beer-Cellars, and there they drink out some Tuns of Beer or Mede ...
Wherein they differ from natural and true Wolves ... Between *Lithuania,*
Samogetia, and *Curonia,* there is a certain left wall, of a Castle that was
thrown down; to this at a set time some thousands of them come together, that each of them may try his nimblenesse in leaping; he that
cannot leap over this wall, as commonly the fat ones cannot, are beaten
with whips by their Captains. And it is constantly affirmed that amongst
that multitude are the great men & chiefest Nobility of the Land."

According to Magnus, a nobleman traveling with many friends

noticed that they were hungry. The band had paused to see a flock of sheep, any one of them able to supply a good supper. Since everyone was aware of the fact that the nobleman was a werewolf, they were not shocked to see him enter a thicket and a wolf emerge. The wolf attacked and killed one of the sheep and left it for the others. Again he entered the thicket and returned as a man to his friends to join in the feast.

The wife of a lord of Livonia denied the possibility of men turning into wolves. One of her servants said that, granted her permission, he would prove that werewolves did exist. In the cellar he made the transformation, but was unfortunately seen by the dogs. The fierce canines blinded one eye with their teeth and the next day the servant appeared before the woman missing an eye.

The Duke of Prussia had, through the powers of a sorcerer, changed himself into a wolf. The nobleman was astonished to see this miracle performed. The Duke had not previously been a believer in witchcraft. To prevent the sorcerer from ever again committing such a terrible sin, the Duke had him burnt to ashes.

HAND OF THE WEREWOLF

The following case of werewolfery was told to Henri Boguet, who actually stayed in the chateau in which it happened. Had he arrived at the chateau two weeks earlier he might have seen the werewolf phenomenon himself.

In 1558, a hunter encountered a friend who was master of a chateau near a village in the hills of Auvergne. Since the huntsman was out for game, his friend asked him to bring back some of the animals he would kill.

The hunter entered a valley, with nothing unusual interfering with his sport. Suddenly a very large wolf appeared and attacked him. In the conflict, the hunter's gun misfired. There was nothing left to do but fight the beast with his knife. Grabbing the creature by the ears, the huntsman cut off one of its furry paws. With the trophy in his hunting bag, the hunter returned to the chateau.

The master of the chateau listened attentively to the hunter's tale and asked to see the severed paw. The hunter opened the bag and found — not the paw of an animal — but, rather, the hand of a woman wearing a gold ring.

The huntsman saw his friend's face pale, for he recognized the ring as one he had bought for his wife. Immediately he went to his wife's room, finding her ill and with a bandaged stump where her hand had been. He confronted her with the truth and she admitted that it was she, in wolf form, that had attacked the hunter.

The woman died soon after and her body was cremated to cleanse it of the werewolf taint.

Shape-Shifting According to Guyon

Guyon writes of various instances of men transforming into beasts.

"Certain people persuaded Ferdiande, first Emperor of that name, to command the presence of a Polish enchanter and magician in the town of Nuremberg to learn the result of a difference he had with the Turks, concerning the kingdom of Hungary; and not only did the magician make use of divination, but performed various other marvels, so that the king did not wish to see him, but the courtiers introduced him into his chamber. There he did many wonderful things, among others, he transformed himself into a horse, anointing himself with some grease, then he took the shape of an ox, and thirdly that of a lion, all in less than an hour. The emperor was so terrified by these transformations that he commanded that the magician should be immediately dismissed, and declined to hear the future from the lips of such a rascal.

"... It need no longer be doubted that Luscious Applies Plato was a sorcer, and that he was transformed into an ass, forasmuch as he was charged with it before the proconsul of Africa, in the time of the Emperor Antonine I., in the year 150 A.D., as Apollonius of Tyana, long before, in the year 60, was charged before Domitian with the same crime. And more than three years after, the rumour persisted to the time of St. Augustine, who was an African, who has written and confirmed it; as also in his time the father of one of Prestantius was transformed into a horse, as the said Prestantius declared. Augustine's father having died, in as short time the son had wasted the greater part of his inheritance in pursuit of the magic arts, in order to flee poverty he sought to marry a rich widow named Pudentille, for such a long time that at length she consented. Soon after her only son and heir, the child of her former marriage died. These things came about in a manner which let people to think that he had by means of magic entrapped

Pudentille, who had been wooed in vain by several illustrious people, in order to obtain the wealth of her son. It was also said that the profound knowledge he possessed — for he was able to solve difficult questions which left other men bewildered — was obtained from a demon or familiar spirit he possessed. Further, certain people said they had seen him do many marvelous things, such as making himself invisible, transforming himself into a horse or a bird, piercing his body with a sword without wounding himself, and similar performances. He was at last accused by one Sicilius OEmilianus, the censor, before Claudius Maximus, proconsul of Africa, who was said to be a Christian, but nothing was found against him.

"Now, that he had been transformed into an ass, St. Augustine regards as indubitable, he having read it in certain true and trustworthy authors, and being besides of the same country; and this transformation happened to him in Thessaly before he was versed in magic, through the spell of a sorceress, who sold him, and who recovered him to his former shape after he had served in the capacity of an ass for some years, having the same powers and habits of eating and braying as other asses, but with a mind still sane and reasonable as he himself attested. And at last to show forth his case, and to lend probability to the rumour, he wrote a book entitled *The Golden Ass*, a melange of fables and dialogues, to expose the vices of men of his time, which he had heard of, or seen, during his transformation, with many of the labors and troubles he had suffered while in the shape of an ass.

"However that may be, St. Augustine in the book of the *City of God*, book XVIII, chapters XVII and XVIII, relates that in his time there were in the Alps certain sorceresses who gave a particular kind of cheese to the passers by, who, on partaking of it, were immediately changed into asses or other beasts of burden and were made to carry heavy weights to certain places. When their task was over, they were permitted to regain their human shape.

"... The bishop of Tyre, historian, writes that in his time, probably about 1220, some Englishmen were sent by their king to the aid of the Christians who were fighting in Holy Land, and that on their arrival in a haven of the island of Cyprus a sorceress transformed a young English soldier into an ass. He, wishing to return to his companions in the ship, was chased away with blows from a stick, whereupon he returned to the sorceress who made use of him, until someone noticed that the ass kneeled in a church and did various other things which only a reasoning being could do. The sorceress who followed him was taken on suspicion before the authorities, was obliged to give him his human form three years after his transformation, and was forthwith executed.

"... We read that Ammonius, a peripatetic philosopher, about the time of Lucius Septimus Severus, in the yards 196 A.D., had present at his lessons an ass whom he taught. I should think that this ass had been at one time a man, and that he quite understood what Ammonius taught, for these transformed persons retain their reason unimpaired, as St. Augustine and other writers have assured us."

WEREWOLF VS. DOGS

In his *Jardin de las Flores curiosas* (1570), Antonio de Torquemada told of a case of werewolfery with a particularly grisly ending.

A warlock, who was also a werewolf, had become quite notorious in Russia. He was, in fact, so infamous that a Russian prince decided that he would put an end to this monster's evil ways.

Sending out his soldiers, the Prince waited until the werewolf was arrested and brought before him. The warlock stood before the Prince, secured by heavy chains.

The Prince was curious to see the transformation about which he had heard so much. Speaking without animosity in his voice, he tricked the warlock into demonstrating his ability to change into a wolf.

Anxiously the warlock agreed, went into a room, and came out in the form of a growling wolf.

But the Prince was all prepared to deal with the werewolf. Immediately he brought into view the two dogs which were trained to kill upon command. Given the command, the fierce canines attacked the werewolf and ripped it to bloody shreds.

15th Century Painting in French manuscript illustrating Marco Polo's "Lykanthropes."

GILLES GARNIER

A letter written by Daniel d'Auge to Matthieu de Challemaison, Dean of the Church of Sens described the infamous *loup-garou* of France, Gilles Garnier:

"This Gilles Garnier, the werewolf *(lycophile)*, was a solitary who took to himself a wife, and them unable to find food to support his family, fell upon such evil and impious courses that whilst wandering about one evening through the woods he made a pact with a phantom or spectral man, whom he encountered in some remote and haunted spot. This phantom deluded him with fine promises, and among other gauds eke taught him how to become a wolf, a lion, and ounce, just as he would list, only advising that since the wolf was the least remarkable of savage beasts this shape would be more conformable. To this he agreed, and received an urgent or salve wherewith he anointed himself when he went about to shift his shape. He died very penitent, having made full confession of his crimes."

Gilles Garnier, born in Lyons, and known as the Hermit of the Dole, was one of the most notorious werewolves of history. He was executed on January 18,1573, but not before his heinous crimes were made public. A document printed at Sens in 1574 stated:

"Anno 1573, on the one part, Henry Camus, Doctor of Laws, Councillor of our Lord the King, in the Supreme court of the Parliament of the Dole, in this case Procurer-General and Public Prosecutor touching the murders committed on the persons of several children and the eating of their flesh in the shape of a werewolf and other crimes and offenses committed by Gilles Garnier, a native of Lyons, now held prisoner in the conciergerie of this town, defendant, on the other part.

"It is proven that on a certain day, shortly after the Feast of St. Michael last, Gilles Garnier, being in the form of a wolf, seized upon in a vinyard a young girl, aged about ten or twelve years, she being in the place commonly called és Gorges, the vinyard de Chastenoy, hard by the Blois de la Serre, about a quarter of a league from Dole, and there he slew and killed her both with his hands, seemingly paws, as with his teeth, and having dragged the body with his hands and teeth into the aforesaid Bios de la Serre, he stripped her naked and not content with eating heartily of the flesh of her thighs and arms, he carried some of her flesh to Apolline his wife at the hermitage of Saint-Bonnot, near Amages, where he and his aforesaid wife had their dwelling.

"Moreover, eight days after the Feast of All Saints last, again being in the form of a wolf, Gilles Garnier attacked another girl in or about the same place, to wit near the meadow called la Ruppe, in the vicinity to Authume, a spot lying between the aforesaid Authume and Chastenoy, and a little before noon of the aforesaid day, he slew her, tearing her body and wounding her in five places of her body with his hands and teeth, with the intention of eating her flesh, had he not been hindered, let and prevented by three persons. This he has several times freely acknowledged and confessed.

"Moreover, some fifteen days after the aforesaid Feast of All Saints, again being in the form of a wolf, having seized yet another child, a boy of ten years old, in a vineyard called Gredisans, at a spot about a league from the aforesaid Dole, situate between the aforesaid Gredisans and Menoté, and having in the same manner as before strangled and killed the aforesaid boy, he ate the flesh of the thighs, legs, and belly of the aforesaid boy, and tore off the body a leg, dismembering it.

"Moreover, upon the Friday before the Feast of St. Bartholomew last he seized a young boy aged twelve or thirteen years under a large pear-tree near the wood which marches with the village of Perrouze in the parish of Cromany, and this young boy he dragged into the said wood, where he strangled him in the same manner as before, with the intention of eating him, which he would have done, had he not been seen and prevented by certain persons who came to the help of the young boy, who was however already dead. The said Gills Garnier was then and at that time in the form of a man and not of a wolf, yet had not be been let, hindered and prevented he would have eaten the flesh of the aforesaid young boy, notwithstanding that it was a Friday.

"Wherefore this Most High and Honorable Court having carefully considered the plea of the Prosecutor, and having made full inquisition into all depositions and interrogatories touching this present case as well as duly weighing the full and free confessions of the accused, not affirmed and deposed once only but many times unambiguously reiterated, acknowledged and avowed, doth now proceed to deliver sentences, requiring the person of the accused to be handed over to the Master Executioner of High Justice, and directing that he, the said Gilles Garnier, shall be drawn upon a hurdle from this very place unto the customary place of execution, and that there by the aforesaid Master Executioner he shall be burned quick and his body reduced to ashes. He is moreover mulcted in the expenses and costs of this suit.

"Given and confirmed at the aforesaid Dole, in the said Court, upon the eighteenth day of the month of January, in the present Year of Grace Fifteen hundred and seventy-three."

PIERRE BURGOT AND MICHEL VERDUN

Jean Bodin related the Sixteenth Century history of werewolves Pierre Burgot and Michel Verdun, who, with a third werewolf, Philibert Montot, were executed and later pictured in the Jacobin Church at Poligny:

"At the parliament of Bezancon, the accused were Pierre Burgot and Michel Verdun, who confessed to having renounced God, and sworn to serve the devil. And Michel Verdun let Burgot to the bord du Chastel Charlon where everyone carried a candle of green wax which shone with a blue flame. There they danced and offered sacrifices to the devil. Ten days after being anointed, they were turned into wolves, running with incredible swiftness; then they were changed again into men, and suddenly transformed back to wolves, when they enjoyed the society of female wolves as much as they had done that of their wives. They confessed also that Burgot had killed a boy of seven years with his wolf-claws and teeth, intending to eat him, but the peasants gave chase, and prevented him. Burgot and Verdun had eaten four girls between them; and they had caused people to die by the touch of a certain power."

WEREWOLVES ACCORDING TO BODIN

Jean Bodin wrote in 1580:

"Pierre Mamor, in a little treaties he has written on sorcerers, says that he has observed this changing of into wolves, he being in Savoy at the time. Henry of Cologne in his treaties *de Lamiis* regards the transformation as beyond doubt. And Ulrich, in a little book dedicated to the emperor Sigismund, writes of the dispute before the emperor, and says that it was agreed, both on the ground of reason, and of the experience of innumerable examples, that such transformation was a fact; and he adds that he himself had seen a lycanthrope at Constance, who was accused, convicted, condemned, and finally executed after his confession. And several books published in Germany say that one of the greatest kings of Christendom, who is not long dead, and who had the reputation of being one of the greatest sorcerers in the world, often changed into a wolf."

Later Bodin added:

"I remember that the attorney-general of the King, Bourdin, has narrated to me another which was sent to him from the Low Countries, with the whole trial signed by the judge and the clerks, of a wolf, which was struck by an arrow on the thigh, and afterwards found himself in bed, with the arrow (which he had torn out), on regaining his human shape, and the arrow was recognized by him who fired it — the time and place testified by the confession of the person."

THE SHEPHERD PETRONIUS

A shepherd name Petronius was tried for werewolfery at Dalheim, Germany, in 1581. In his work *Compendium Maleficarum* (1608), Francesco Maria Guazzo stated:

"Whenever he felt moved with hatred or envy against the shepherds of neighboring flocks (as is the way of such men) he used to change himself into a wolf by the use of certain incantations, and for so long a time escaped all suspicion as being the cause of the mutilation and death of his neighbors' sheep."

WEREWOLVES BURNED AT THE STAKE

The penalty in France for werewolfery was often burning at the stake. A number of confessed werewolves were tried in court, convicted and disposed of in that gruesome manner.

A huge, tailless wolf had attacked sixteen-year-old Benoist Bidel of Naizan and his younger sister while they were picking wild fruit one day in 1584. The local peasantry heard the commotion and dashed to the childrens' aid. The boy was already dead, but there was yet a chance to save his sister from so ghastly a fate. The peasants vengefully descended upon the brute, mortally wounded it, and watched it limp into the bushes. Instead of finding a wolf in that thicket, the peasants were confronted with the corpse of Perrenette Gandillon.

It was later discovered that Perrenette came from a family of sorcerers and werewolves. Her brother Pierre and son George were proven to have anointed themselves with an ointment that transformed them into wolves. In wolf form, they had attacked and devoured too many children to note.

According to Henri Boguet, the members of this family walked about on all fours, had sharp, wolflike nails, and very lupine faces — with matted hair, red eyes, and sharp white fangs. They were Satanists and from the Devil received the secret of the ointment.

The careers of these two werewolves ended at the fires of the stake. In 1598, a number of witches in France were convicted of being werewolves. Members of the Orcieres coven, including Clauda Jamguillaume, Thievenne Paget, and their notorious leader Clauda Jamprost, all admitted to prowling the forest of Froidecombe as werewolves. Satan had told them how to make the ointment, they confessed, as he did the warlock Jacques Bocquet.

Clauda Jamprost repented and was the first of the group to suffer the flames; the others soon followed.

More witches, accused of being werewolves, were likewise burned at the stake, including a woman named la Micholette, and in July of that year, Francoise Secretin.

Bocquet himself accused Francoise of being a werewolf. Beforehand, she admitted to having used her witchcraft to kill human beings and cattle and to having sexual intercourse with Satan in his guise of a black man. Francoise denied that she was also guilty of werewolfery.

Perhaps one of the most grisly cases of a werewolf who was eventually sent to the stake was that of a tailor in Paris. Not only did he lure children of both sexes to his shop and molest them, slicing their throats and dressing their corpses like sides of beef, but he also became a wolf at dusk and bit through the throats of people who had the misfortune of encountering him.

When his house was searched the cellar was discovered to be filled with such items as barrels of human bones.

The tailor never repented, even as flames of the stake consumed him. To erase the details of the case from history, the Court burned the documents concerning it as well.

In 1604, according to Jean Nynauld's *De La Lycanthropie*, five werewolves were burned at the stake at Lausanne.

These sorcerers worked their evil spells from the nearby village of Cressi. When they needed a child to sacrifice at their sabbat, they transformed themselves into wolves and kidnapped one that suited their purposes. The poor victim was killed by the fiends, who then drank the child's blood and devoured the severed parts of the body. These were indeed resourceful werewolves, for even the child's fat was used in the making of their ointments.

STUBBE PEETER

A *German* (called *Peter Stumpe*) by charme,
Of an inchanted Girdle, did much harme,
Transforms'd himselfe into a Wolfeish shape,
And in a wood did many years escape
The hand of Iustice, till the Hang-man net him,
And from a Wolfe, did whit an halter set him:
Thus counterfaithing shapes haue had ill lucke,
Witness *Acteon* when he plaid the Bucke ...

The preceeding verse from *The Knave of Hearts* (1612), by Samuel Rowlands, refers to the most infamous werewolf of Germany, Stubble Peeter (also known as Peter Stumpf, Stump, Stub and Stube). Stubbe Peeter was executed by the State at Bedburg on March 31, 1590, for his crimes as a werewolf. The full account of the fiend was given in a pamphlet issued at the time, the only known existing copies now in the Lambeth Library and the British Museum:

A true Discourse
Declaring the damnable life
And death of one Stubbe Peeter, a most
Wicked Sorcerer, who in the likeness of a
Woolfe, committed many murders, continuing this
Diuelish practice 25. Years, killing and de-
Vouring Men, Woman, and
Children.
Who for the same facet was taken and executed the 31. Of October
Last past in the Towne of Bedbur
Neer the Cittie of *Collin.*
In *Germany.*

Trulye translated out of the high Duch, according to the Copie printed in Collin, brought over into England by George Bores ordinary Poste, The xj. Daye of this present Moneth of June 1590. Who did both see and heare the same.

AT LONDON
Printed for
Edward Venge, and are to be
Solde in Fleet-street *at the signe of the*
Vine.

A most true Discourse,
Declaring the life and death of one
Stubbe Peeter, being a most
Wicked Sorcerer.

Those whome the Lord dooth leaue to followe the Imagination of their own hartes, dispising his proffered grace, in the end through the hardness of hart and contempt of his fatherly mercy, they enter the right path to perdicion and destruction of body and soule for euer: as in this present historie in perfect sorte may be seen, the strangeness whereof, together with the cruelties committed, and the long time therein continued, may driue may in doubt whether the same be truth or no, and the ratherfore that sundry falce & fabulous matters haue heertofore passed in print, which hath wrought much incredulitie in y harts of all men generally, insomuch that now a daise fewe things doo escape be it neuer so certain, but that it is embased by the terms of a lye or falce reporte. In the reading of this story, therefore I doo first request information of opinion, next patience of puruse it, because it is published for examples sake, and lastly to censure thereof as reason and wisdome dooth think conueniet, considering the subtilty that Sathan vseth to work the soules destruction, and the great matters which the accursed practise of Sorcery dooth effect, the fruites whereof is death and destruction for euer, and yet in all ages practised by the reprobate and wicked of the earth, some in one sort and some in another euen as the Deuill giueth promise to perfourme. But of all other that euer lived, none comparable vnto this hellhound, whose tiranny and cruelty did will declare he was of his Father the deuill, who was a murderer from the beginning, whose life and death and most bloody practises the discourse following dooth make iust reporte. In the townes of Cperadt and Bedbur neer vnto Collin in high Germany, there was continually brought vp and nourished one Stubbe Peter, who from his youth was greatly inclined to euill, and the practising of wicked Artes euen from twelue years of age till twentye, and so forwardes till his dying daye, insomuch that surfeiting in the Damnable desire of magick, negromancye, and sorcery, acquainting him selfe with many infernall spirites and feendes, insomuch that forgetting y God made him, and that the Sauiour that shed his blood for mans redemption: In the end, careless of saluation gaue both soules and body to the deuil for euer, for small carnall pleasure in this life, that he might be famous and spoken of on earth, though he lost heauen thereby. The Deuill who hath a readye eare to listen to the lewde motions of cursed men, promised to give vnto him whatsoeuer his hart desired during his mortall life; whereupon this vilde wretch neither desired riches nor promotion, nor was his fancy satisfied with any externall or outward pleasure, but hauing a tirannous hart, and a most cruell bloody mine, he only requested that at his plesure he might woork his mallice on men, Women, and children, in the shape of some beast, whereby he might liue without dread or danger of life, and vnknown to be the executor of any bloody enterprise, which he meant to commit: The Deuill who sawe him a fit instruemet to perfourm mischeefe as a wicked feend pleased with the desire of wrong and destruction, gaue vunto him a girdle which being put about him, he was straight mighty, with eyes great and large, which in the night sparkeled like cruell teeth. A huge body, and mightye paws: And no sooner should he put off the same girdle, but presently he should appeere in his former shape, according to the proportion of a man, as if he had neuer beene changed.

Stubbe Peter heerwith was exceedingly well pleased, and the shape fitted his fancye and agreed best with his nature, being inclined to blood and crueltye, therefore satisfied with this strange and diuelish gifte, for that it was not troublesome nor great in cariage, but that it might be hidden in a small room, he proceeded to the executions of sundry most hainous and vilde murders, for if any person displeased him, he would incontinent thirts for reuenge, and no sooner should

they or any of theirs walke abroad in the feeldes or about the Citties,
but in the shape of a Woolfe he would presentlye incounter them,
and neuer rest till he had pluckt out their throates and teare their
ioyntes a sunder: And after he had gotten a taste heerof, he tooke
such pleasure and delight in shedding of blood, that he would night
and day walke the Feelds, and work extreame cruelties. And sundry
times he would goe through the Streetes of Collin, Bedbur, and
Cperadt, in comely habit, and very ciuilly as one will knowen to all
the inhabitants thereabout, & oftentimes was he saluted of those
whose freendes and children he had buchered, though nothing suspected for the same. In these places, I say, he would walke vp &
down, and if he could spye either Maide, Wife or childe, that his
eyes liked or his hart lusted after, he would waite their issuing out of
y Cittie or town, if he could by any meanes get them alone, he
would be in the feeldes rauishe them, and after in his Wooluishe
likenes cruelly murder them: yea often it came to passe that as he
walked abroad in the feeldes, if hi chaunste to spye a company of
maydens playing together, or else a milking of their Kine, in his
Wooluishe shape he would incontinent runne among them, and
while the rest escaped by flight, he would be sure to laye holde of
one, and after his filthy lust fulfilled, he would murder her presentlye,
beside, if he had liked or knowne any of them, look who he had a
mind vnto, her he would pursue, whether she were before or behinde,
and take her from the rest, for such was his swiftness of foot while
he continued a woolf: that he would outrun the swiftest greyhound
in that Countrye: and so muche he had practiesed this wickedness,
that y whole Province was feared by the cruelty of this bloody and
deuouring Woolfe. Thus continuing his diuelishe and damnable
deedes within the compas of fewe years, he had murdered thirteene
yong Children, and two goodly yong women bigge with Child, tearing the Children out of their wombes, in most bloody and sauedge
sortie, and after eats their hartes panting hotte and rawe, which he
accounted dainty morsells & best agreeing to his Appetite.

Moreouer he used many times to kill Lambes and Kiddes and
such like beastes, feeding on the same most vsually raw and bloddy,
as if he had beene a naturall Woolfe indeed, so that all men mis-
trusted nothing lesse than this diuelish Sorcerie.

He had at that time liuing a faire yong Damosell to his Daughter, after whom he also lusted most vnnaturallye, and cruellye committed most wicked inceste with her, a most groce and vilde sinne,

far surmounting Adultry or Fornication, though the least of the
three dooth driue the soule into hell fier, except hartye repentance,
and the great mercy of God. This daughter of his he begot when he
was a not altogither so wickedlye giuen, who was called by the name
of Stubbe Beell, whose beautye and good grace was such as deserued
commendacions of all those that knewe her: And such was his inordinate lust and filthye desire toward her, that he begat a Childe by
her, dayly vsing her his Concubine, but as an insaciate and filthy
beast, giuen ouer to woork euil, with greedines he also lay by his
owne Sister, frequenting her company long time euen according as
the wickedness of his hart lead him: Moreouer being on a time sent
for to a Gossip of his there to make merry and good cheere, ere
thence departed he so wunne the woman by his faire and flattering
speech, and so much preuailed, y ere he departed the house: he lay
by her, and euer after had her company at his commaund, this woman
had to name Katherine Trompin, a woman of tall and comely stat-
ure of exceeding good favour and one that was well esteemed among
her neighbours. But his lewed and inordinate lust being not satisfied with the the company of many Concubines, nor his wicked
fancye, contented with the beauty of any woman, at length the deuill
sent vnto him a wicked spirit in the similitude and likeness of a
woman, so fair of face and comelye of personage, that she resembled
rather some heavenly Helfin than any mortall creature, so fair her
beauty exceaded the choisest sorte of woman, and with her as with
his harts delight, he kept company the space of seuen years, though
in the end she proued and was found indeed no other than a she
Deuil, notwithstanding, this lewd sinne of lecherye did not any thing
asswage his cruell and bloody minde, but continuing an insatiable
bloodsucker, so great was the icye he took therein, that he accounted
no day spent in pleasure wherein he did not shed some blood not
respecting so much who he dooth manifest, which may stand for a
speciall note of a cruell and hard art. For hauing a proper youth to
his sonne, begotten in the flower and strength of his age, the firste
fruite of his bodye, in whome he took such ioye, that he did commonly call him his Hartes ease, yet so farre his delight in murder
exceeded the ioye he took in his only Sonne, that thirsting after his
blood, on a time he inticed him into the feeldes, and from thence
into a Forrest hard by, where making excuse to stay about the neces-
saries of nature while the yong man went on forward incontinent in
the shape and likeness of a Woolfe he encountered his own Sonne,

and there most cruelly slewe him, which doon, he presently eat the
brains out of his head as a most sauerie and dainty delycious meane
to staunch his greedye apetite: the most monstrous act that euer
man heard off, for neuer was knowen a wretch from nature so far
degenerate.

Long time he continued this vilde and villanous life, sometime
in the likeness of a Woolfe, sometime in the habit of a man, sometime, in the Townes and Citties, and sometimes in the Woods and
thickettes to them adioyning, whereas the duche coppye maketh
mention, he on a time mette with two men and one woman whom
he greatly desired to murder, and the better to bring his diuelish
purpose to effect, doubting by them to be ouematched and knowing
one of them by name, he vsed this pollicie to bring them to their
end. In subtill sorte he conuayed himselfe far before the min their
way and craftely couched out of their sight, but as soone as they
approached neere the place where he lay, he called one of them by
his name, the partye hearing him selfe called once or twice by his
name, supposing it was some familiar freend that in iesting sorte
stood out of this sight, went from his companye towarde the place
from whence the voice proceeded, of purpose to see who it was, but
he was no sooner entered within the danger of this transformed
man, but incontinent he was murdered in y place, the rest of his
company staying for him, expecting still his returne, but finding his
stay ouer long : the other man lefte the woman, and went to looke
him, by which means the second man was also murdered, the woman
then seeing neither of both returne againe, he hart suspected that
some euill had fan vpon them, and therefore with all the power she
had, she sought to saue her selfe by flight, though it nothing preuailed,
for good soule she was also soone ouertaken by this light footed
Woolfe, whom when he had first deflowred, he after most cruelly
murdered, the men were after found mangled in the wood, but the
womans body was neuer seene, for she the caitife had most
rauenouslye deuoured, whose flesh he esteemed both sweet and dainty
in taste.

Thus this damnable Stubbe Peeter liued the tearme of fiue and
twenty yeeres, unsuspected to be Author of so many cruell and
vnnaturall murders, in which time he had destroyed and spoyled an
vnknown number of Men, Women, and Children, sheepe, Lambes,
and Goates: and other Cattell, for whom he could not through the
warines of people drawe men, Women, or Children in his danger,

then like a cruell and tirannous beast he would woorke his cruelty on brut beasts in most sauadge sort, and did act more mischeefe and cruelty then would be credible, although high Germany hath been forced to take the trueth thereof.

By which means the inhabitantes of Collin, Badbur and Cperadt, seeing themselues so greeuously endaungered, plagued, and molested by this greedy and cruel Woolfe, who wrought continuall harme and mischeefe, insomuch that few or none durst trauell to or from those places without good prouision of defence, and all for feare of this deuring and fierce woolf, for oftentimes the Inhabitants found the Armes and legges of dead Men, Woman, and Children, scattered vp and down the feelds to their great greefe and vexation of hart, knowing the same to be doone by that strange and cruell Woolfe, whome by no means they could take or ourcome, so that if any man or woman mist their Childe, they were out of hope euer to see it again aliue, mistrusting straight that the Woolfe had destroyed it.

And here is to be noted a most strange thing which setteth foorth the great power and mercifull prouidence of God to y comfort of eache Christian hart. There were not long agoe certain small Children playing in a Medowe together hard by y town, where also some store of kine were feeding, many of them hauing yong calues sucking upon the: and sodainly among these Children comes this vilde Woolfe running and cought a prittie fine Girle by the choller, with intent to pull out her throat, but such was y will of God, that he could not pearce the choller of the Childes coate, being high and very well stiffened & close claspt about her neck, and therwithall the sodaine great crye of the rest of the childre which escaped, so amazed the cattell feeding by, that being fearfull to be robbed of their young, they altogether came running against the Woolfe with such force that he was presently compelled to let goe his holde and to run away to escape y danger of their hornes, by which means the Childe was preserued from death , and God be thanked remains liuing at this day.

And that this thing is true, Maister Tice Artine a Brewer dwelling at Puddlewharfe, in London, beeing a man of that Country borne, and one of good reputation and account, is able to iustifie, who is neere Kinsman of this Childe, and hath from thence twice receiued Letters concerning the same, and for that the firste Letter did rather driue him into wondering at the act then yeelding credit there therunto, he had shortlye after at request of his writing another letter sent him, wherby he was more fully satisfied, and diuers other persons of great credit in London hath in like sorte receiued letters from freends to the like effect.

Likewise in the townes of Germany aforesaid continuall praier was vsed vnto god that it would please him to delieuer the from the danger of this greedy Woolfe.

And although they had practised all the meanse that men could deuise to take this rauenous beast, yet vntil the Lord had determined his fall, they could not in any wise preuaile: notwithstanding they dayle continued their purpose, and dayle sought to intrap him, and for that intent continually maintained great mastyes and Dogges of muche strength to hunt & chase the beast whersoeuer they could finde him. In the end it please God as they were in readiness and prouided to meete with him, that they should espye him in his wooluishe likeness, at what time they beset him round about, and most circumspectlye set their Dogges vpon him, in such sort that there was no means to escape the imminent danger, being hardly pursued at the heeles presenly he slipt his girdle from about him, wherby the shape of a Woolfe cleane auoided, and he appeered presently in this true shape and likeness, hauing in his hand a staffe as one walking toward the Cittie, but the hunters whose eyes was stedfastly bent vpon the beast, and seeing him in the same place metamorposed contrary to their expectation: I wrought a wonderfull amazement in their mindes, and had it not beene that they knewe the man so soone as they sawe him, they had surely taken the same to haue beene some Deuill in a mans likeness, but for as much as they knewe him to be a ancient dweller in the Towne, they came vnto him, and talking with him they brought him by communication home to his owne house, and finding him to be the man indeede, and selusion or phantasticall motion, they had him incontinent before the Maiestrates to be examined.

Thus being apprehended, he was shortly after put to the racke in the Towne of Bedbur, but fearing the torture, he volluntarilye confessed his whole life, and made knowen the villanies which he had committed for the space of xxv. yeeres, also he confessed how by Sorcery he procured of the Deuill a Girlde, which beeing put on, he forthwith become a Woolfe, which Girdle at his apprehension he confest he cast it off in a certain Vallye and there left it, which when the Maiestrates heard, they sent to the Vallye for it, but at their coming found nothing at al, for it may be supposed that it was gone to the deuil from whence it came, so that it was not to be found. For the Deuil hauing brought the wretch to al the shame he could, left him to indurethe torments which his deeds deserued.

After he had some space beene imprisoned, the maiestrates found out through de examination of the matter, that his daughter Stubbe Beell and his Gossipp Katherine Trompin, were both accessarye to diurse murders committed, who for the same as also for their leaud life otherwise committed, was arraigned, and with Stubbe Peeter condempned, and their seuerall Iudgenentes pronounced the 28 of October 1589, in this manor, that is to saye: Stubbe Peeter as principall mallefactor, was iudged first to haue his body laid on a wheele, and with red hotte burning pincers in ten seueral places to haue the flesh puld off from the bones, after that, his legges and Armes to be broken with a wooden Axe or Hatchet, afterwards to haue his head strook from his body, then to haue his carkasse burnde to Ashes.

Also his Daughter and his Gossip were iudged to be burned quicke to Ashes, the same time and day with the carkasse of the aforesaid Stubbe Peeter. And on the 31. Of the same moneth, they suffered accordingly in the town of Bedbur in the presence of many peeres & princes of Germany.

Thus Gentle Reader haue I set down the true discourse of this wicked man Stub Peeter, which I desire to be a warning to all Sorcerers and Witches, which vnlawfully followe their owne diuelish imagination to the vtter ruine and destruction of their soules eternally, from which wicked and damnable practice, I beseech God keepe all good men, and from the crueltye of their wicked hartes. Amen.

After the execution, there was by the aduice of the Maiestrates of the town of Bedur a high pole set vp and stronglye framed, which first wentthrough y wheel wheron he was broken, whereunto also it was fastened, after that a little aboue the Wheele the likeness of a Woolfe was framed in wood, to shewe unto all men the shape wherein he executed those crueltyes. Ouer that on top of the stake the sorcerers head it selfe was set vp, and round about the Wheele there hung as it were sixteen pieces of wood about a yarde in length which represented the sixteen persons that was perfectly knowen to be murdered by him. And the same ordained to stand there

For a continuall monument to all insuing ages, what murders by Stub Peeter was committed, with the order of his Iudgement, as this picture doth more plainelye espresse.

Witnesses that is
true
Tyse Artnye
William Brewar
Adolf Staedt
George Bores.
With diuers others that haue seen the same.

Wolves with Human Hands and Feet

Not all werewolves transform in the same way. While some men assume the shape of a wolf others change into a monstrous combination of man and wolf. Some of these combinations seem to be unique, as in the two cases of wolves with human hands and feet as described by Henrie Boguet in his *Discours des Sorciers* published in 1590.

Clauda Gaillard and Jeanne Perrin were strolling through the woods with the alms they had collected that day. Jeanne was satisfied with her alms, but Clauda kept grumbling that she did not have enough. She was still complaining when she left her friend and dashed into the bushes.

Jeanne looked curiously toward the bushes. Surely not having enough alms was not a good reason for her curious actions. She waited for her friend to settle down and come back apologizing for her strange behavior.

The creature that sprang from the bushes was not capable of apologizing for anything. It was a huge wolf with human toes on its hind feet.

Jeanne Perrin was so terrified she could only flee the monster, taking the time to make the Sign of the Cross and drop her alms.

Everyone assumed from Jeanne's story that the werewolf was her friend Clauda. Clauda confirmed the suspicion when she confided in Jeanne that the wolf would not have hurt her. Clauda's confidence left little doubt that she did not go into those bushes to count her money again or to answer the call of nature.

A similar case involved teenaged Benoist Bidel, who had gone out with his younger sister to pick fruit. Spying some fruit in a tree, he climbed the tree while his sister watched him.

The bushes stirred. The girl quickly turned to see a terrible monster emerge from the foliage. The Creature was a large wolf — or almost a wolf. The body was definitely lupine, but the forefeet were like hairy human hands.

Benoist watched as the wolf attacked his sister. With an incredible burst of speed, he jumped to the ground and threw himself upon the beast, stabbing away with his knife.

The battle of man against monster was a furious one, the wolf having the advantage. With a lash of one of its arms, the monster stabbed the knife into Benoist's neck. Then the animal reacted to the sounds of people rushing upon the violent scene. The beast could not withstand the blows of the mob, but before it fled into underbrush, it left the boy fatally wounded.

Benoist's bleeding body was taken to his father's house. He was barely alive but was able to describe the beast that had maimed him. His strange story told, Benoist Bidel died.

Finding the person responsible for the attack was a simple matter. Perrenette Gandillon, a local witch, was found to be hurt in exactly the same fashion as the wolf. There was little she could say in her own defense, and the villagers dealt with her accordingly.

LYCANTHROPE IN CHURCH

A case attributed to a lycanthrope was included in Pierre van Forest's (1552-97) *Observationum ... Medicinae Theoricase et Practicae Libri XXVIII.* Van Forest was a famous Dutch physician in the town of Alkmaer. The portion of his text concerning the church-going of lycanthrope is *De lycanthropia seu lupina insania* in the tenth book *De Cerebri Morbis.*

During the spring, a peasant was roaming through the streets of Alkmaer as though he were motivated by the instincts of an animal. His face was twisted into the angry snarl of a beast and there was no look of intelligence in his eyes. As passersby noticed the strange man, he instinctively avoided them.

Van Forest observed the actions of the man and diagnosed him to be an authentic lycanthrope.

The man was not under the care of any doctor whom van Forest knew and so he decided to follow the lycanthrope.

Unlike the vampire who shuns the cross and other religious articles, this man growled and sprang into a nearby church, unaware that van Forest was following him.

Although he took the precaution of remaining in hiding, van Forest could see that the man's skinny body showed signs of neglect, as if he had been truly living the existence of a beast. His flesh was filthy and covered with sores and the bites of animals. His eyes seemed to blaze, making him appear even more inhuman. He clutched a club in one hand, which he had been using to fight off the dogs of Alkmaer.

That was the creature van Forest watched in the church. Before van Forest could stop him, the lycanthrope had already mingled with the citizenry of Alkmaer and fled to safety.

Jacques Roulet

One day in 1598, Symphorien Damon, an archer of the Provost's company, was in a wild area near Caude at Angers. He and some people who lived in the area were aghast at what they found lying in the grass. It was the mangled corpse of a boy about fifteen years-old, still throbbing with its last moments of life.

All felt a sense of nausea as they looked about for the killer, possibly still making his escape from the scene of the murder. Running into the distance they saw a pair of wolves, undoubtedly responsible of the terrible slaughter.

Taking their weapons, the rustics, led by Damon, hurried after the brutes. What they encountered startled even the bravest of them. It was a tall, thin man clothed in dirty rags. His hair was long and matted, his eyes blazing red, his sharp fingernails scarlet with blood.

The stranger, who identified himself as Jacques Roulet, was taken before the magistrate. He was recognized as a vagrant who, with his brother Jean and cousin Julien, often roamed from one village to the next in the hopes of securing handouts.

Jacques Roulet fully confessed to the Maître Pierre Hérault, the *lieutenant général et criminel,* on August 8th. His parents, he said, had acquired a salve for changing into a wolf from Satan, to whom he had been dedicated. As a wolf, he would experience unholy desires that were easily satisfied. Jean and Julien were the two wolves who had evaded Damon and the rustics in the woods.

Roulet's confession was extremely detailed. His knowledge of the times and locations of the various attacks were so accurate that there was not doubting his guilt. He gave an especially vivid description of his slaying of a child near Bournaust whom he attacked, like the others, with his fangs and claws, and whose flesh he had devoured.

He also admitted to being a Devil-worshipper who frequently attended the unholy rites.

Jacques Roulet had confessed enough to warrant him the burning stake. He was condemned to die, yet he escaped death. The Parliament of Paris instructed that he be kept in the hospital of Saint Germain-des-Prés, where he spent most of his time snarling and howling like a wolf.

JEAN GRENIER

Pierre de Lancre included his meeting with *loup-garou* Jean Grenier in his work *Tableaus de l'Iconstance des Mauvais Anges et Demons* (1613).

The werewolf had escaped the death penalty for his horrendous crimes because of his youthful ignorance and was confined to the Franciscan monestary of St. Michael the Archangel. The creature called Jean Grenier seemed barely human.

The boy looked at him with burning eyes. Occasionally he would walk on all fours with the agility of a wolf, snapping about with his claw-like nails and white fangs. He preferred raw meat and delighted in conversing about his favorite subject — wolves.

A creature believed to be a werewolf had been terrorizing the St. Severs districts of Gascony in 1603. Children were being kidnaped, even from their cradles, by some fiend who moved with the stealth and silence of an animal.

The belief in a *loup-garou* in the vicinity was strengthened when teenaged Marguerite Poirier swore that she had been attacked by a monstrous wolf beneath the light of the full moon. The monster would have killed her had she not been able to fight it off with an iron pointed staff.

Hardly anyone doubted the existence — or identity — of the *loup-garou* when Jean Grenier, a boy of thirteen or fourteen years, bragged that Marguerite's stick was the only thing that stopped him in wolf form from devouring her.

On another occasion, Grenier admitted to eighteen year-old Jeanne Gaboriaut that he was a member of a coven of nine werewolves. Donning belts made of wolf skin, they would transform on Mondays, Fridays, and Saturdays, hunting in the forests and fields at twilight and before sunrise. He preferred the tender flesh of children, especially favoring the thighs, Grenier said.

On May 29th these confessions were in the hands of the authorities. Grenier's verbosity had proven his downfall. He was arrested and taken to court on June 2nd where he revealed the startling facts in his case.

After running away from an unloving father who constantly beat him, Grenier encountered a young boy named Pierre de la Tilhaire. One evening the boy took Grenier into the woods where he met a dark man on a black horse, identified as the Lord of the Forest. First, the Lord saluted the boys; then he implanted an icy kiss on Grenier's lips and rode into the shadows of the woods.

Grenier encountered the Lord of the Forest on another occasion. This time the Lord gave him the power to transform himself into a wolf. In the shape of a large feline, the Lord showed Grenier a salve and wolf's skin, which the boy could borrow any time he desired to make the transformation. The one stipulation was that he never cut his left thumb nail. It must grow into a crooked claw.

Jean Grenier enjoyed his life as a werewolf, adding to his menu the flesh of a three-year-old girl named Guyonne, whom he killed on the First of March, and the child of Jean Roullier, whose older son fought off the fiend.

After his arrest, Grenier implicated his father, accusing him of witchcraft and werewolfery. After some rather brutal interrogation, Pierre Grenier was proven innocent and totally ignorant of Jean's life as a *loup-garou.*

Jean Grenier's trail was held by the Parliament of Bordeaux on September 6, 1603. But unlike most werewolves, Grenier was not sentenced to death by President Dassis.

The friars at the monastery watched over their strange inmate. Their work was somewhat successful, as he reported that when the Lord of the Forest had twice visited him, he fled as Grenier crossed himself. In November of 1611, Jean Grenier died in that friary of St. Michael the Archangel.

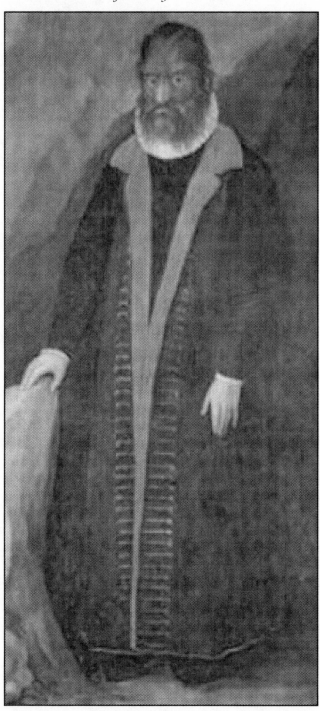

*16th Century
Portrait of
Petrus
Gonsalvus –
A possible
werewolf?*

WEREWOLF
IN THE MUSEUM

In 1685 in the town of Ansbach, Bavaria, a werewolf was said to be plaguing the vicinity, attacking animals and even human beings. When the corpse of the burgomaster was discovered it was the consensus of the townspeople that he was the werewolf that had been devouring their woman and children.

The beast into which the burgomaster had allegedly transported his spirit was eventually killed. The more artistic people of the town prepared it with flesh colored cloth, a wig, a suit of clothes, and even a mask, making the carcass resemble the dead burgomaster.

The bizarre creation was stuffed and exhibited in a museum as "proof" that a werewolf really existed.

KIDNAPED
BY LYCANTHROPES

Thomas Bird, in his *History of the Royal Society of London* (1756-57), stated that on September 2, 1663, Sir Kenelm Digby at a meeting of the Royal Society ... read a letter, sent to him out of the Palatinate, concerning some children snatched away in those parts by beasts, that had the appearance of wolves; but found killed after so strange a manner, that all people thereabout surmised, that they were not wolves, but *lycanthropi*, seeing that nothing of the bodies of those children were devoured, but the heads, arms, and legs, severed from their bodies, the skulls opened, and the brains taken out and scattered about the carcases, and the heart and bowels, in like manner, pulled out, but not devoured."

THE DUKE
AND THE LYCANTHROPE

A case of lycanthropy appeared in *Dies Caniculares* (1691) by Simone Maiolo, Bishop of Volterra, happening only a few years earlier.

For over a year, the Duke of Muscovy had observed his prisoner, curious to see if he would make good his boast. The prisoner claimed that he was a werewolf who had transformed into a beast-man every year at Christmas and at, approximately, the Feast of St. John the Baptist. On those days he was supposedly seized by the feeling that he was becoming a wolf. Then he would hurry to the woods where hair would sprout over his whole body.

The man was apprehended in the act of devouring the Duke's cattle which he had slain in the manner of a wolf. Covered with the teeth-marks of dogs and deformed and ugly to see, the man confessed to the Duke that he was indeed a werewolf.

The Duke, wishing to learn if the man's confession were true, imprisoned him. But, on the days he was supposed to make his transformation, there occurred no change. The lycanthrope's self-claimed metamorphosis was apparently the product of his own insanity.

MÈRE MAXIM

Werewolfery has often been inflicted upon a person as a form of revenge. One such case, reported during the Eighteenth Century, took place in a village three miles from Bolis, France.

Beatrice, the pretty daughter of an innkeeper named Antonio Cellini, was in love with a handsome young man named Herbert Poyer. But a homely young man, Henri Sangfeu, also loved the young woman. If not for a hag of the village writing a poem entitled *Sansfeu the Ugly; or, Love Unrequited*, which caught on in the village, Henri might not have decided to take revenge upon Beatrice. The girl whom he loved now recited the poem loudest. Now he hated her as much as he had previously loved her.

In the heart of the forest lived Mère Maxim, believed to be an old hag of a witch who was not afraid to take human lives when it suited her. On a bright morning, Henri visited the witch and learned, to his delight, that she was a quite attractive young woman with a warm complexion and long raven hair. The two were attracted to each other and were soon making love.

Henri was overweight and was too infatuated with the woman to be affected by the way she pinched him and said she liked fat men.

Seeking revenge, Henri told Mère Maxim what he wanted. She guaranteed that he would have his revenge providing he follow her instructions implicitly and tell no one of his visits.

The witch handed Henri a belt made from the skin of some beast and fastened with a buckle of gold. This, along with a box of candy, was to be Beatrice's wedding present, given on the eve of her marriage.

Back in the village, Henri could think only of his coming vengeance and his feelings for the witch. He no longer heard the jeers of the villagers who taunted him with the poem and references to his unsightly long nose.

Seeming to have no animosity toward Beatrice or her bridegroom, Henri gave her the strange belt and candy on the eve of the wedding. Then he waited, patiently. Before long, he saw a hairy, dark shape jumping from one tree to the next. A face, possibly that of an animal or some grotesque human being, stared at him from the branches of an enormous oak tree. He ran away from the tree, noticing that the shape leapt to the ground and then ran off into the night.

When Henri returned to Mère Maxim, the witch did a peculiar thing. She remarked again on how delightfully fat he was. Then, waiting until he became intoxicated and unable to resist, she bound him with ropes so tightly that he could not break free. Helplessly he watched her rip open his shirt to expose his throat and chest.

Staring hungrily at Henri, the witch told him that by donning the belt and eating the candy she had become a werewolf. Every midnight she would she would assume an animal shape and go off in search of human victims.

Henri Sangfeu had gotten his revenge, a little love, and something he had not figured in the deal. Mère Maxim was already drooling and making the transformation into the beast over which she had such obvious powers.

THE MARE-WOMAN

Dom Augustin Calmet wrote of a curious incident involving a woman believed to have changed into a horse.

"One day there was brought to St. Macarius, the Egyptian, an honest woman who had been transformed into a mare by the wicked art of magician. Her husband and all who beheld her believe that she had really been changed into a mare. This woman remained for three days without taking any food, whether suitable for a horse or for a human being.

"She was brought to the priests of the place, who could suggest no remedy. So they led her to the cell of St. Macarius, whom God had revealed that she was about to come. His disciples wished to send her away, thinking her a mare, and they warned the saint of her approach, and the reason for her journey. He said to them: 'It is you who are the animals, who think you see which is not; this woman is not changed, but your eyes are bewitched.' As he spoke he scattered holy water on the head of the woman, and all those present saw her in her true shape. He had something given her to eat and sent her away safe and sound with her husband."

THE WILD BEAST
OF GÉAUDAN

Le Géaudan is a particularly rugged mountain area of France. Around the year 1764, that vicinity was terrorized by a horrible monster known simply as the Wild Beast of Géaudan, an enormous wolf-like creature able to destroy even groups of men with its teeth, talons, and tail, capable of leaping and running with unnatural energy, and leaving in its wake a foul odor.

The London Magazine, or Gentleman's Monthly Intelligencer (1765) reported:

"... a detachment of dragoons has been out six weeks after him. The province has offered a thousand crowns to any persons that will kill him."

The Wild Beast spared no age or sex. On July 8, 1764, it tore the heart from a young girl near the town of St. Etieene de Lugdares, ate it and drank her blood. The monster seemed to develop a taste for the flesh of children and killed five more that same week. On the evening of January 15, 1765, the Wild Beast killed a fourteen-year-old shepherd named Jean Chateauneuf in the same gory fashion. The monster disappeared amid the shadows before the vengeful father could fire his gun.

In his *Correspondance Littéraire* of April 1, 1765, Baron Friedrich Melchior von Grimm wrote:

"For several months now the *Gazette de France* has been chronicling exploits of a new kind, for it never misses to give us an extraordinary recital of this ferocious beast in the Géaudan, and loudly praises the heroic and memorable feast of those who take the field against the monster."

Grimm also praised the actions of eleven-year-old Andre Protefaix, who, on January 20, 1765, had heard his young friends being attacked by the Wild Beast. Armed only with a pitchfork, he fought off the monster until the other villagers were able to drive it into the hills.

Hardly anyone believed anymore that the Wild Beast was just an overgrown wolf. The monster seemed to have a particular craving for the flesh of girls, which made people suspect that it was a *loup-garou* or werewolf.

In *Court Magazine* (1838), Sutherland Menzies wrote:

"I remember to have seen an engraving in which that animal was represented devouring a girl, and subscribed Lycopardus Parthenophagus, vulgb *La BLte de Géaudan*. Parthenophagy, or a peculiar delight in the flesh of girls, is an enormity of the lycanthropes and not of wolves; from which we may infer in what light the people in the Géaudan regarded that famous beast."

On February 6, the Wild Beast was tracked by a dragoon sent by King Louis XV to a plateau. The soldiers blasted away at the shadowy, growling figure. The monster howled from the agony of its wounds, then vanished amongst the thickets, apparently to die. Shortly after, the supposedly dead monster had gorged itself on another victim.

The entire countryside was both infuriated and living in terror. Nothing seemed able to destroy the Wild Beast which became bolder with every passing day. People were in danger even while behind their locked doors.

Thousands of people had attempted to kill the monster, no one being successful.

As the climax of the story, there are two versions. Montague Summers, in *The Werewolf*, attributes the death of the Wild Beast of Géaudan to a Monsieur Antoine.

Warren Smith, however, provided a more glamorous ending in his book, *Strange Monsters and Madmen.*

An elderly hunter named Jean Chastel prayed for help in slaying the monster, then loaded his double-barreled musket with silver bullets. Aiming his weapon at the heart of the creature, he blasted away. He could not afford to miss.

Chastel examined the lifeless carcass of the Wild Beast and noted that it resembled both man and wolf with peculiar hoofed feet. Tradition says that the actual remains of the monster were too ghastly to see, so another dead wolf was exhibited in the towns. Whether it was a particularly large wolf or was in fact a werewolf, the vicinity was never again plagued by the Wild Beast of Géaudan.

SCANDINAVIA'S WEREWOLVES

Among the Scandinavian stories of werewolves, it is often difficult to distinguish those intended as pure fiction from those reputed to be fact.

An ancient Norse story involved two werewolves asleep in their house while the wolf-shirt responsible for their transformations hung on the wall. Sigmund the Volsung and his son Sinfjötli came upon the two sleepers and, enticed by the wolf-shirts, donned them. For the next ten days they became wolves, prowling through the forests enjoying their brutal lives as animals. After the spell ended they burned the shirts, thankful to be human again.

The *Volsunga saga* includes the story of an old she-wolf that continuously devoured human beings. Most everyone believed that the mother of King Siggeir had used magic to transform herself into the murderous beast.

In the year 1808, according to Arvad August Afzelius' *Svenska Folk-Visor Fran Forntiden* (1814-16), a Swedish soldier from Calmar came home from the war with Russia somewhat inhuman. He had somehow gained the ability to transform into a wolf, making him a *Varulf* or *Man-ulf.* When the wolf was shot to death and skinned, the shirt of the soldier was found next to the carcass.

WOLF HOLLOW

During the early 1800s, count Von Breber, the chief of police of Magdeburg, Germany, and his beautiful young wife Hilda, were traveling through the Harz Mountains.

A strange thing happened to them on their way to the village of Grautz. The Count and Countess came upon a brook over which their dogs were most reluctant to cross.

Later at an inn of the village, the Countess told what had happened to the innkeeper. When she described the brook with its two giant poplar trees, the innkeeper paled. That was Wolf Hollow, he said, the waters of which had a strange effect upon anyone drinking them.

The Count would hear no more of this nonsense, especially since his wife had drunk the water and would undoubtedly be upset by the tale. The innkeeper, threatened by the Count with flogging and having his tongue cut out, wisely agreed to keep the story to himself.

Once Von Breber and his wife returned to their estate, Hilda began to act queerly. Weird dreams, which she kept to herself, began to haunt her. Her eating habits became poor and she was starting to physically decline. The Count, feeling that it would be better to leave her alone for a while, took the bedroom next to hers.

Count Von Breber had enough worries when the unexplainable disappearance of children put the vicinity in an uproar. Despite the number of men he put on guard in the town, the children, mostly from poorer homes, mysteriously vanished. It was a simple matter to quiet the poorer parents when they complained. But it was impossible to hush up Meichen, the banker who lost his three-year-old daughter and Otto Schmidt, who lost a six-year-old daughter.

The Count knew he had to change his tactics when General Carl Rittenberg a very important man in the province, told how his child Elizabeth had vanished from him when they momentarily parted in the fog of Frederick Street. The General was extremely irate and threatened to destroy thoroughly the Count's name unless he saved his child from the unknown kidnapper.

Immediately Count Von Breber went to work, having his men search every street in Magdeburg. He was in his home worrying over the situation when a woman stormed through the door. She was Martha Brochel, half-mad over the loss of her child, claiming that the kidnapper was not human but a terrible monster of the night.

The Count did not believe her ravings and sent her out into the street. But thinking there might be some truth to her story, he followed her. Ahead of Martha was a dark form, seemingly a woman, carrying a sack over one shoulder. Martha exclaimed that this was the fiend who had taken her child. Then she, with the Count in fast pursuit, ran after the woman.

The chase was so furious that the Count did not recognize the ground over which he ran. He was exhausted, fell and bruised himself, while Martha's energy seemed renewed. There was a building not too far distant. The fiend hurried inside the house with Martha bolting in after her. Von Breber shuddered as he heard Martha's screams mingled with the snarls of a wild beast and the noises of crunching bones.

After a terrible silence settled over the house, Count Von Breber breathed deeply and slammed in the door. Pieces of human corpses lay in all corners of the room. On the ground, with face mangled and breast and abdomen torn open, was what remained of Martha.

Crouched over the mass of gore was a monstrous werewolf, with the shapely body of a woman, with long blond hair, and the head, feet, and bloody hands of a wolf.

The werewolf growled, then turned to escape into the night. Count Von Berber knew that his position demanded that the monster not escape. He squeezed the handle of his sword and drove the entire length of the blade into the creature's back.

The Count shut his eyes as the werewolf fell to the floor. Something was happening that he knew it would be better not to behold. At last he opened his eyes, then felt sick. Lying before him, with his sword protruding from her back, was his beloved wife Hilda. He was standing in his own summerhouse on his own property, which she had been using as a base of gruesome operations and dining room.

Before Hilda died she confessed that it was the water she drank in the Harz Mountains that transformed her into a beast.

WEREWOLF WITH EVIL EYES

Tam McPherson, an old man of a village at the bottom of Ben MacDhui, had known a villager named Saunderson — a man who had long been suspected of being a werewolf.

McPherson described Saunderson as "a mon with evil leerie eyes, and eyebrows that met in a point over his nose." These were traditional identifying characteristics of a werewolf.

Saunderson had acquired more suspicion on himself by his choice of residence. He lived in a cave in the mountains, once the home of his ancestors. They too were believed to have transformed into wolves.

After Saunderson died, a band of villagers went to his cave to search the place, hoping to find some evidence proving his ability to change his form.

It was said that bones of both men and wolves were found in the musty cave, some of which had been covered with dirt like graves.

THE VARGAMOR

Vargamores are creatures, similar to werewolves, that inhabit the forest of Sweden. Although they do not assume the shape of wolves, they have total control over these beasts and often delight in sharing their meals.

Liso of Soroa was a vain wife and the mother of three children. When her aunt at Skatea wrote requesting that she and the children come out for a visit, Liso complied.

During the ride through the forest, Liso's magnificent horse panicked as a pack of hungry wolves appeared on the road. Liso drove her animal harder, but the wolves continued snapping and snarling. In a short while the horse would fill their respective bellies.

Liso did not want to lose the horse, especially since she would then also lose her own life. There was nothing to do but sacrifice her children, she reasoned, one by one, which occupied the wolves while she drove toward a nearby house.

Inside the house, Liso was confronted by a old hag. The wolves were at the window and still hungry. The old woman said that she was a Vargamor and would feed Liso to her wolves unless she remained to do the housework for the rest of her days.

Liso took the job. When she tried to escape, the wolves drove her back to the house. One day the inevitable happened. The wolves and the hag were hungry and, unless Liso provided a substitute victim to feed them, she would satisfy their hunger. Liso guaranteed that she would find a substitute and immediately wrote a letter to her doting husband Oscar.

Oscar arrived at the old house. While the Vargamor was summoning the wolves, Liso killed her, then grabbed Oscar's hand and led him to his coach. Within moments the coach was taking Liso and her husband back toward civilization when, again, the wolves appeared in a reenactment of Liso's previous predicament.

At first, Liso contemplated hurling the driver to the wolves as she had done with her children. But her horrible experiences were effecting her conscience. The coachman was married and had three children. She, however, now had no children. By hurling herself to the half-starved beasts, Liso surmised, she might atone for her past sin.

When she told her husband what she planned to do, he forbade the suicidal act, showing that he possessed enough weapons to keep back the wolves.

The coach was drawn out of the ominous woods. Liso finally mustered the courage to tell Oscar what had happened to their three children. She finally felt true love for her man and thought it best that he know everything.

However, Oscar looked with contempt upon the woman, calling her a murderess and a fiend. Although she finally realized her love for Oscar, it was too late. She was worse than the Vargamor that she had killed. Liso would spend the rest of her life in the home of her parents.

PETER ANDERSEN

Peter Andersen was descended from a long line of Danish werewolves. When he fell in love with a beautiful young girl named Elisa, he thought it best not to tell her of his hereditary affliction. He married her and prayed for the best.

The newlyweds were coming home from a village fair one evening when Peter experienced strange sensations. The werewolf metamorphosis was about to take place.

He quickly told the girl not to be afraid of anything that she might see out of the ordinary. If anything menaced her, she should merely strike the offender with her apron.

Leaving Elisa to hold the horses, Peter ran into the fields. Shortly after, Elisa heard the howl of a wolf and saw a large gray beast springing at her.

Elisa did as Peter had instructed her. Taking off her apron, she struck the wolf in the face. The monster snapped off a piece of the apron and then ran off. Later, Andersen in his human form presented her with the piece of cloth.

Peter Andersen then told his wife that by striking him with the apron, she forever ended his werewolf curse. He begged her forgiveness and Elisa granted it.

A similar case also is reported from Denmark, but with less successful results. A haymaker, who had not told his family that he was a wolf-man, felt the change affecting him and told his son to hurl his hat at any approaching animal, striking it. When the boy saw a gray wolf swimming the stream, he attacked it with a pitchfork, impaling the heart. Everyone looked with horror as the dead wolf metamorphosed into the corpse of the haymaker.

IVAN
OF SHIGANSKA

Ivan of Shiganska, a small village that existed until about 1870 a hundred miles from the mouth of the Petchora, was a skilled hunter and a fisherman whose main love was the hunt.

One morning in April, Ivan, accompanied by his faithful dog Dolk, went hunting reindeer in the magnificent forest near his home. Ivan and his dog chased after a beautiful reindeer. But when the hunter caught up with his fleet running companion, he saw something that angered him greatly. Dolk was being bitten in half by a white wolf. When the lupine brute saw Ivan, it fled, leaving the remains of an animal that had been a true friend to the hunter and his family.

Revenge was Ivan's only thought. He followed the tracks of the wolf to a dark cavern. As he walked through the rocky chamber he heard not the howl of a wolf, but the laughter of a woman. He turned and saw an incredibly lovely young woman with golden hair, gleaming white teeth, and long, pointed fingernails.

The girl, name Breda, had met a true romantic. Ivan would not leave her alone, began to court her, and soon took her to the altar of matrimony.

Ivan's mother and sister did not like Breda. She was often a dominating sort and preferred raw meat to cooked. It seemed ominous that, some weeks after she moved into the house, a wolf, whose tracks always led to Ivan's home, began killing off the neighbors' horses and cattle.

The wolf killings also effected Ivan's family. One by one his sisters were found killed as though by wolves, with their bellies torn open and flesh devoured. Ivan's mother was already suspecting that their tragedies were the result of a supernatural fiend. She would be the next to die.

Ivan awakened to the sounds a growls and screams coming from his mother's room. Taking his gun and running to the room, he saw a giant wolf with white fur gnawing on his mother. Ivan fired a bullet into the monster but it was too late to save his mother. Her throat and body had already been slit open.

He followed the trail of blood into Breda's room where, to Ivan's horror, he found his wife wounded in the shoulder by a bullet that fit the bore of this own weapon. She could do nothing more than confess that she became a werewolf voluntarily by eating a certain lycanthropous blue flower in order to kill her sadistic first husband.

The villagers were already suspecting Breda of werewolfery. There was talk that they would soon disinter and examine the body of Ivan's mother who, supposedly, had died from heart failure.

Desperate, Ivan consulted an old metaphysician and sage, who said that the only answer to the situation was exorcism. This would be better than death by a violent mob.

There was a full moon when Breda transformed into a white wolf and Ivan, the old man, and three assistants crept into her room and subdued the beast. Outside, the old sage placed the beast inside an equilateral triangle drawn into the dirt, kindled a fire, and heated over it a concoction of vinegar, hypericum, cayenne, sulphur and mountain ash berries.

Ivan watched with fascination as the old man did these things. But he could not tolerate what was to happen next. After prayers had been said and the noxious fumes of the mixture rose into the moonlit heavens, the old metaphysician and his helpers cut switches of mountain ash and prepared to flog the werewolf spirit out of the white wolf. Enraged, Ivan seized the whips and began to lash the three men, who ran from the place screaming in pain.

Smiling, Ivan knelt before the white wolf and cut its bonds. The beast stared at him with her gray eyes, then started to move away. The thing that had been the girl Breda gave him a final look and then vanished amongst the distant trees.

A Family of Werewolves

A peasant woman named Martha was appalled when her child returned home, bleeding and bruised, with the story that a certain Madame Tonno had taken the child to her home, where she and her children transformed into wolves and prepared to devour its tender flesh. The child would be eaten the next day, for there was still the remains of another corpse to be finished.

The story of Madame Tonno presented a problem to Martha and her husband Max. Hers was a wealthy and prominent family and one just did not go about accusing a Tonno of werewolfery.

Martha was washing the family's clothes in a tub when she heard her child scream. A large she-wolf had her child in its jaws and was carrying it away. Martha managed to grab onto the child's clothing, ripping off a piece of cloth as the wolf escaped with its juicy prize.

It was a simple matter to follow the monster. Pieces of clothing and human hair lined the trail. There were always screams of her child to drive her onward until she, too, fell prey to the cravings of the she-wolf.

When Max discovered the mangled body of his wife, he went to the Tonno house and confronted the master, demanding justice for the loss of Martha and his child to Mr. Tonno's werewolf spouse. Mr. Tonno invited him inside and promptly imprisoned him in a room with barred windows.

Max knew that he would be werewolf food unless he escaped. Luckily he found that the floorboards were loose and managed to move under the house and escape by pulling out the grating.

At first the peasants of Lapland did not believe Max' story of the Tonno werewolves. When more of the children of the neighborhood also vanished, however, the peasants gathered up their pitchforks and swords and stormed the chateau of the werewolves. They were efficient in battering down the door and seizing the family of man-eaters, binding them, and throwing them in the waters of Lake Enara where they were drowned.

THE WEREWOLF SECRET

The son of a resident of Lynbrook, New Jersey, discovered something strange in 1967. It was a "wooden box with brass bindings, about six by six inches, with a family crest on the top and a key inside," according to the New York *Daily News*.

The box was judged to be approximately two hundred twenty-three years old by the Samuel Richards Galleries in Lynbrook. According to the experts at the Galleries, the receptacle was probably made in Siebenburgen.

A letter dated 1823 and written in German was found in a secret compartment of the box.

The following is stated in the *Daily News*.:

"It was written by a half-crazed man about to commit suicide. He says he had been bitten by a wolf one lonely nigh earlier and each month thereafter turned into a werewolf, fled into the woods and stalked human prey. Filled with despair, and unable to find escape, he has chosen death ..."

From Wagner the Wer Wolf,

PRINCE BIORNO, THE WERE-BEAR

The following narrative by Sir Walter Scott appeared in *The History of Hrolfekraka:*

Hringo, king of Upland, had an only son, called Biorno, the most beautiful and most gallant of the Norwegian youth. At an advanced period of life, the king became enamoured of a "witch-lady" whom he chose for his second wife. A mutual and tender affection, had, from infancy, subsisted betwixt the youth Biorno and Bera, the lovely daughter of an ancient warrior. But the new queen cast upon her stepson an eye of incestuous passion; to gratify which, she prevailed upon her husband, when he set out on one of those piratical expeditions, which formed the summer campaigns of a Scandinavian monarch, to leave the prince at home.

In the absence of Hringo, she communicated to Biorno her impure affection, and was repulsed with disdain and violence. The rage of the weird stepmother was boundless. "Hence to the woods." She exclaimed, striking the prince with a glove of woolskin; "Hence to the woods! Subsist only on thy father's herds; live pursuing and die pursued!"

From this time the prince Biorno was no more to be seen and the herdsman of the king's cattle soon observed that astonishing devastation was nightly made among their flocks by a black bear of immense size and unusual ferocity. Every attempt to snare or destroy this animal was found vain; and much was the unavailing regret for the absence of Biorno, whose one delight had been in extirpating beasts of prey.

Bera, the faithful mistress of the young prince, added her tears to the sorrow of the people. As she was indulging her melancholy, apart from society, she was alarmed by the approach of a monstrous bear, which was the dread of the whole country. Unable to escape, she waited its approach in expectation of instant death; when to her astonishment, the animal fawned upon her, rolled himself at her feet, and regarded her with eyes, which, in spite of the horrible transformation, she still recognized as the glances of her lost lover. Bera had the courage to follow the bear to his cavern, where during certain hours, the spell permitted him to resume his human shape.

Her love overcame her repugnance at so strange a mode of life, and she continued to inhabit the cavern of Biorno, enjoying his society during his periods of freedom from enchantment. One day, looking sadly upon his wife, "Bera," said the prince, "the end of my life approaches. My flesh will soon serve for the repast of my father and his courtiers. But do thou beware lest either the threats or entreaties of my diabolical stepmother induce thee to partake of the horrid banquet. So shalt thou safely bring forth three sons who shall be the wonder of North."

The spell now operated, and the unfortunate prince sallied forth from the cavern to prowl among the herds. Bera followed him weeping, and at a distance. The clamor of the chase was now heard. It was the old king, returned from his piratical excursions, who had collected a strong force to destroy the devouring animal which ravaged his country. The poor bear defended himself gallantly, slaying many dogs, and some huntsmen, At length, wearied out, he sought protection at the feet of his father. But his supplicating gestures were in vain, and the eyes of paternal affection proved more dull than those of love. Biorno died by the lance of his father, and his flesh was prepared for the royal banquet.

Bera was recognized and hurried into the queen's presence. The sorceress, as Biorno had predicted, endeavored to prevail upon Bera to eat of what was then esteemed regal dainty. Entreaties and threats being vain, force was, by the queen's commands, employed for this purpose, and Bera was compelled to swallow one morsel of the bear's flesh. A second was put into her mouth, but she had a opportunity of putting it aside. She was then dismissed from her father's house.

Here, in process of time, she was delivered of three sons, two of whom were affected variously in person and disposition by the share their mother had been compelled to take in the feast of the king. The eldest from his middle downwards resembled an elk, whence he derived the name Elgfrod. He proved a man of uncommon strength, but of savage manners, and adopted the profession of a robber. Thorer, the second son of Bera, was handsome and well shaped, saving that he had the foot of a dog; from which he obtained the appellation of Houndsfoot. But Bodvear, the third son, was a model of perfection in mind and body. He revenged upon the necromantic queen the death of his father, and became the most celebrated champion of his age.

Werewolves of the Harz Mountains

During the summer of 1840, two men named Hellen and Schiller were walking in the Harz Mountains. When Schiller sprained his ankle, he bade his friend go on, confidant that he would soon encounter a woodcutter or charcoal-burner. Although he disliked leaving his friend, Hellen continued on his hike.

Hellen began to worry about his friend when he heard the cry of a wolf. Neither of the men possessed weapons. A more terrible feeling coursed through Hellen when he found himself walking toward a clearing surrounded by pines, traditionally an evil haunt.

A man was sitting on the ground bandaging his wrist. When Hellen offered his assistance, the man said that his name was Wilfred Gaverstein and that he had broken his wrist when he fell from a tree, where he had been hiding from a wolf. Hellen helped bind the man's wrist, then told of Schiller. Wilfred offered both of them the hospitality of his home.

As the two men approached the house, Hellen described his wife and three little girls, to the delight of Wilfred. In return for describing his family, Wilfred told Hellen how he worshiped only nature. As a wolf again began to howl in the vicinity, Hellen quickened his pace.

When Wilfred's cottage finally came into view, Hellen gasped. The cottage was in the image of his own home. Hurrying inside the house, he was astonished to find his entire family there, all of whom claimed to have been in Frankfort only moments before. Hellen could explain nothing to his wife and children who wished only to go home.

Wilfred Gaverstein provided Hellen and his family with many comforts. For Hellen himself there seemed to be an added comfort. When he first beheld Wilfred's gorgeous daughter, Marguerite, he desired her. The blonde young woman was only twenty years old, clad in fur and buckskin. Moreover, there was something mysterious about her, something exotic, that despite his attempts, Hellen could not resist.

He had never been unfaithful to his loving wife. But there was something bewitching about this Marguerite.

The children had gone to bed and were kissed and patted by Marguerite who eyed them strangely. She suggested that Hellen accompany her into the woods. It was time they looked for Schiller, she said. During the trek through the forest, Hellen could think only of the beauty at his side. The only thing that changed his thoughts was his discovery of Schiller, now a half-eaten, mutilated corpse. Schiller's death was apparently the work of wolves.

For a while Hellen thought only of what had happened to his friend. Then he was again seized by his longing for Marguerite and, unable to control himself, began to kiss her. At first she protested, but then said he could have her, if he wished, on the enchanted clearing in the woods. He was permitted two wishes. His first wish was to have Marguerite; the second, to have her forever.

As they returned to the cottage, Hellen heard his wife and children screaming for help. He rushed forward to assist them, but was tripped by Marguerite, who reminded him of his second wish. He fought to escape, but her grip was like a vise. When the horrible screams ceased to emanate from the house, Marguerite released her grip. Bolting into the house, Hellen saw that he was too late. Lying upon the floor, chests and throats ripped open, were Hellen's wife and children. Leering at him with a sadistic grin was Wilfred Gaverstein.

Grabbing an axe from the wall, Hellen attacked Wilfred. The axe passed harmlessly through Wilfred's body and Hellen realized that he was dealing with phantoms of the Harz mountains — ghostly werewolves.

Marguerite tore out a lock of her yellow hair and stuffed it into Hellen's hand, then scratched his forehead with her sharp nail. She would return to him when that mark began to heal. With that, Hellen fell into unconsciousness.

When Hellen awakened he was lying alone in the middle of the haunted circle of pines. For a few moments he was thankful that his dreadful experience had only been a dream. Then he felt sick, for in his hand was the tuft of golden hair placed there by Marguerite.

When Hellen told an innkeeper what had happened, he was informed that Wilfred and Marguerite were notorious werewolves who periodically visited the area.

Armed and burning for revenge, Hellen marched back to the place where the cottage had been. This time, he vowed, Wilfred and Marguerite would fall victims to his bullets. None of the villagers would accompany him for fear of the werewolves. But it did not matter, for this was Hellen's private war with the supernatural.

To his amazement, there were no signs of a cottage ever being in the spot he knew it had been.

When Hellen returned to his home in Frankfort he was confronted with more tragedy. His wife and children had been discovered in their beds, their chests torn open and their throats ripped out. Despite his attempts to attribute the case to coincidence, there was still that handful of blonde hair and the wound on his forehead.

The wound completely healed on the day of Hellen's death.

SERGEANT BERTRAND

Although his case is usually attributed to vampirism, Sergeant Bertrand clearly fits into the category of werewolf.

Paris was in a panic in 1847. An unknown fiend was creeping into graveyards at night with the stealth of an animal, disinterring corpses, and devouring the dead flesh. What was described as a creature part man and part beast was sometimes seen springing amid the shadowy gravestones. The creature howled and barked like an animal, but always seemed to vanish when pursued.

Everyone seemed under suspicion of being the mysterious werewolf or vampire that was molesting the corpses. The caretakers of the graveyards, the police, and even the relatives of the deceased were all suspected and questioned. Nothing seemed capable of stopping the monster since its first such act in the Cemetery of Père Lachaise. Doctors were summoned to examine the partially eaten corpses in their open coffins or strewn about the ground, and all agreed that the teeth marks were made by a man.

People were arrested, but no one was proven to be the ghoulish fiend. The public more fervently demanded a satisfactory arrest when the body of a newly buried little girl was dug up and devoured. The girl's father was arrested, but proven to be innocent.

An army officer offered his help to stop the creature. Skilled in explosives, he rigged a charge to erupt on the ten-foot-high wall of a certain graveyard. The culprit had to only touch the wire that ran the length of the wall. And no one could climb over that wall without touching the wire.

A group of detectives waited in the darkness until an ape-like creature bolted through the graveyard and, evading their bullets, sprang for the wall. As he reached the top of the wall, he was caught in the explosion and then escaped over the other side.

The police now had a clue as to the identity of the fiend. Blood was splashed amidst pieces of a torn soldier's uniform. Finding a recently wounded soldier was hardly difficult, especially when some members of the 74th Regiment said that a severely wounded sergeant had just been taken to the hospital of Vel de Grâce.

Sergeant Bertrand, it was learned, was guilty of mysteriously disappearing from his post on many occasions. When confronted by the police, Bertrand freely admitted that some external power forced him to rip into corpses and gorge himself on human flesh. Fifteen bodies in one night were not too many for Bertrand. The Sergeant described how, like a hungry animal, he dug up the corpses with his hands. When he did this, he added, he was no longer a man but, rather, a savage animal.

In court, Sergeant Bertrand revealed more of his life and the incidents that drove him to become what he was. As a child he preferred animals to human beings and kept them company in isolated places wherever he could. One evening, after having been in the company of animals, he happened upon some grave diggers in the act of covering up a body. Fascinated by the coffin, Bertrand stared at it, all the while trying to suppress a desire to devour the contents. From then on, he was never able to control the foul desires and simply submitted to them.

Sergeant Bertrand was examined by doctors, all of whom said that he was totally sane. His strange behavior was attributed to his obsession with corpses. Bertrand was tried and sentenced to one year in prison. Upon his release he went into self-exile and was never heard from again.

VICTIM OF LYCOREXIA

Lycorexia (or lycorrhexis) is the term given to a particularly wolfish hunger suffered by certain lycanthropes.

A lycanthrope with this hunger had been under the care of a Dr. Morel. The man's story was included among the cases in Morel's *Études Cliniques* in 1852. The case is also cited by Dr. Daniel Hack Tuke in his *Dictionary of Psychological Medicine,* volume ii (1892).

Although the poor lycanthrope did not physically transform into an animal, he believed that he did. He would frequently show Dr. Morel his teeth which, in his mind, were truly sharp fangs.

"See this mouth," he would tell the doctor. "It is the mouth of a wolf. These are the teeth of a wolf."

Dr. Morel would watch and take notes as his patient described the other parts of his body that were, in reality, quite human.

"I have cloven feet. See the long hairs which cover my body."

Naturally there were no long hairs.

"Let me run into the woods and you shall shoot me!"

Some of the lycanthrope's visitors were children, who came to him and even embraced him when he was not raving about being an animal. But he continued raving after they had gone.

"The unfortunates!" he exclaimed. "They have hugged a wolf!"

The lycanthrope's favorite food was served to him upon his demand.

"Give me raw meat! I am a wolf! A wolf!"

Given the raw meat, the unfortunate man would gorge himself and then discard what was too fit for human consumption. He was a wolf, he claimed, and no wolf would accept meat that was too fresh.

The lycanthrope was committed to the asylum of Maréville where he continued to confess to the most ghastly crimes, all supposedly perpetrated while in the shape of a wolf. What was most tragic is that he was innocent of the crimes regardless of his shape.

The man continued to waste away, both physically and spiritually, until he died in the asylum, still certain that he was a werewolf.

Montague Summers, in his book *The Werewolf*, attributes the case to diabolical possession.

BRIDE OF THE WEREWOLF

Paul Nicholas was perturbed as he sat in his room at *l'Hôtel Hervada* in the September of 1853. He was a rich and handsome bachelor whose main desire was the beautiful young woman who had recently taken the room next to him. Unfortunately, he was unable to possess her, for she seemed to have a preference for other men.

All of the tenants of the hotel were talking about the mysterious beauty. She would often be seen in the company of an overweight middle-aged man, go off with him for any length of time, and then, surprisingly , return alone.

Paul was too hopelessly in love to think anything ill of the woman. He determined to win her over, first by purchasing a guitar, composing love songs, and then singing them to her. He learned that her name was Isabelle de Nurrez. But even though Paul sang to her, Isabelle found herself another fat man of considerable years.

The guests at the hotel complained to the manager, since the woman was obviously of questionable morals. But she was paying more to stay at the hotel than all the other guest combined. The manager was not going to evict such a tenant.

Paul wrote Isabelle a letter expressing his true feelings for her. At last she responded and invited him to her hotel room. She looked even more beautiful now since she was dressed with many ornaments of glittering gold.

Isabelle told Paul a fantastic story regarding her life. According to the beauty, her father, recently deceased, had met a young Hindu named Prince Dajarah while a voyage in the Mediterranean for his health. He would leave Isabelle all of his wealth providing she marry the Prince.

In those days a Caucasian marrying a black man could be considered a serious offense. And so Isabelle fled with the Prince in vengeful pursuit. She explained that the men with whom she left the hotel had agreed to kill the Prince. But when they had seen the tall black man they ran away with fear.

If Paul truly loved her, she said, he would perform the assassination. After some deliberation, Paul agreed to shoot Prince Dejarah.

The coach bearing Paul Nicholas and Isabelle de Nurrez was soon traversing the wilds of Spain, with barren trees and enormous boulders that made him uneasy. Looking up at the driver, Paul recognized him as a notorious Spanish bandit. A stench of decay permeated the area. Their destination, a gray house with vacant windows and surrounded by the white trunks of rotten trees, was already in sight.

Paul complained, but Isabelle said that she was reluctant to describe the house for fear that he would not have come. She reminded him of his vows to kill her tormentor.

Isabelle kissed him and then led her would-be rescuer through the catacomb-like passageways of the house. The walls were barren, the rooms cold like a tomb, which reminded Paul of a structure built in a nightmare world. All the while he felt that something was lurking in the darkness, ready to leap out and attack him.

She led him to a small room, empty save for a marble table over which was suspended a single oil lamp. The Prince would soon be there, she assured him.

Isabelle asked to see Paul's weapons — a pistol and a knife — which she took from him for examination. When he wanted them back to use against the Prince, she refused, laughing at the latest fool to believe her lies. The story about her father and the Prince was completely untrue. The man she married was not a black man or a prince — but a werewolf.

During certain days of the year he would only eat human flesh. And so Isabelle used herself as bait to lure love-struck men, with lots of meat on their bones, to her husband's banquet table.

While she was speaking, the door opened and her husband, a handsome soldier, entered the room. He smiled as he looked at his latest juicy victim. Then he warned his wife to leave the room, for he felt the transformation about to begin.

Isabelle de Nurrez left Paul Nicholas alone with her husband and closed the door. She grinned upon hearing the sounds of violence and the final screams of the victim. That night her husband would not go to bed hungry.

Le Meneur Des Loups

The *Le Meneur des Loups* was a wizard of France and Brittany, whose greatest delight was to lead a pack werewolves on their terrible hunts. Since he knew the area, he was able to tell the werewolves the best places and times to strike, often joining them in the shape of a wolf with a human mind and voice. "Le grand Julien" of Saint-Aôut, master of the musette, was such a being, living during the early 1800s.

George Sand relates instances involving *Le Meneur der Loups* in the *Légendes Rustiques* (1858).

An aged verderer stood in the open space of a forest, waving his hands in the air, as though making signals. He was observed by two men who were hiding in a tree. They were surprised to see that, answering the verderer's summons, were numerous wolves, led by an enormous gray beast that caressed the old man as a faithful dog would its master. Then the man led the wolves into the forest, chanting as he vanished amid the thick vegetation.

A similar occurrence took place in the Forest of Châteauroux. Two men walking through the woods began to run as they heard the sound of a wolf behind them. A tree offered them protection. Climbing the tree, the two wayfarers peered through the branches to witness a pack of growling wolves stop before the hut of a woodman. The beasts continued to snarl and howl until the man within opened the door. He patted their furry hides and spoke to them. At last the animals became calm as if acknowledging the rustic as their master.

"I know several persons," writes Sand, "who at the first faint rising of the new moon have met near the carfax of the Croix-Blanche old Soupison, nicknamed Démmone, walking swiftly along with great giant strands followed in silence by more than thirty wolves."

THE ISAWIYYA

During the 1860s, a certain European was repulsed when he witnessed the lycanthropic behavior of a Moslem sect called the Iiswiyya.

The initiates to the sect were engaged in a wild dance, with which they became frenzied and seemingly possessed by the spirits of animals. As they moved they made noises like beasts and foamed at the mouth. The ceremony climaxed with their falling to the ground, writhing with convulsions as bowls of reptiles, scorpions, and toads were placed before them. Each of the wriggling little creatures attracted the new members of the Isawiyya. Their eyes, enflamed with madness, as they grabbed up the snakes and lizards and other prey from the bowls and devoured them alive.

The Isawiyya was founded by Ibn Isa, an Arab mystic of the late Fifteenth and early Sixteenth Centuries. According to tradition, Ibn Isa was the master of the demons and lesser creatures of the Earth. His followers wore masks of such animals as jackals, lions, panthers, dogs, cats, camels and boars, colored their hands red to simulate blood, and enacted the roles of wild beasts. A highlight, during a ceremony, was to kill an animal and gulp down the bloody flesh.

Ostensibly, the Isawiyya is a religious sect primarily concerned with a love for God.

Today the Isawiyya have members in the Sudan, Middle East, and North Africa.

WEREWOLVES RELATED BY D'ASSIER

In his *Posthumous Humanity,* Adolphe D'Assier attributed two strange occurrences to werewolfery.

A creature resembling a calf appeared in the bedroom of two brothers in 1868 at Saint-Lizier. The brothers awoke to see the strange apparition. In the name of God they told it to depart, at which time the calf passed through the door and was heard outside of the room on the stairs. The older brother said that the animal was actually a resident of the town and was believed to be werewolf.

Bigot, a Miller moonlighting as a warlock, lived at Serisols in the Canton Sainte-Croix. His wife left him in bed one morning in 1879 in order to do the washing in the backyard. An animal resembling a large dog stood at one end of the yard and was so menacing in appearance that the woman was determined to drive it off. Quickly, she took a piece of wood and slammed the creature in the eye.

Simultaneously, Bigot awoke, holding his eye and shrieking to the consternation of his children:

"Wretch, you have blinded me!"

From then on Bigot wore an eyepatch

JOANA OF TARCOUÇA

Joana of Tarcouca, in the mountains of Beira, was both a witch and a werewolf who spread her evil through Portugal. The account of this monster was related by Oswald Frederick Crawfurd in 1870, published in John Latouche's *Travels in Portugal* in 1873.

One of the most savage districts of Portugal was Estrica. A young farmer (who told the story to Crawfurd in later years) had disregarded warnings to stay out of the area and took employment at a farm near Cabrasa, located in the Estrica mountains. Since the wife of the master of the farm was pregnant, the farmer decided to hire someone to perform the work about the house.

The young farmer was sent to Ponte de Lima, the closest town, to find a suitable woman. He encountered a young woman in a brown cloak sitting by the road. She identified herself as Joana from the Tarcouca in the Beira mountains. Furthermore, she was looking for such a domestic job and eagerly accepted the position at the farm.

The child was born, normal except for a peculiar indelible mark in the shape of a crescent or half moon between the baby's shoulder blades. An old woman, known for her wisdom, reacted with horror, saying that this was the mark of the Devil and that the child should be watched during the cycle of the new moon. The parents did as she instructed, but nothing happened to validate the woman's fears.

Joana seemed to be terrified of the old woman and always managed to be engaged in work in a different room when she came into the house. If there was no work to do, Joana would hide in the shadows, her great cloak concealing her blazing eyes and wolfish expression.

Furthermore, Joana confided in her mistress that the child would grow up to be a *lupis-homens* unless certain precautions were taken before he reached the age of sixteen.

"You must cover the mark with the blood of a white pigeon," said

Joana, "strip the child naked, and lay him on a soft blanket on the mountain-side when the very first new moon rises in the heavens after midnight. Then the moon will draw the mark up through the blood, just as she draws the waves of the sea, and the spell will be broken."

After conferring with each other, the parents did as Joana instructed, leaving their child alone on the slope of a nearby hill under the new moon.

There were no wolves in the area. Nevertheless the farmer felt a terrible apprehension that his child was in danger of his life. Grabbing his blunderbuss, he hurried out to the slope where he saw a sickening tableau. An enormous brown wolf was standing over the mangled body of his son. The monster's fangs were scarlet and its eyes ablaze.

Firing his weapon, the father wounded the beast, while his young hired man tried to kill it with a club. The monstrous wolf managed to limp into the darkness, but not before the farmer saw the eyes of Joana staring at him from the lupine face.

When the corpse of the boy was taken back to the house, Joana was the only one not present. At dawn she was found lying outside, wounded from a blunderbuss and club, exactly as the wolf had been. She did not confess, but stated that in order to protect the child from the wolf she inadvertently ran into the farmer's line of fire. No one believed her story, for the old woman discovered the sign of the Devil on her breast, branding her a *lobis-homens*. Such a werewolf, she said, can break the charm which binds it by killing a newly born child and consuming its blood.

The farmer sent for a priest but Joana died before he arrived.

Crawfurd says, "... the superstitions have the peculiar gloomy stamp of the legendary mysteries of ancient Italy .... The type of Latin legend to which I refer, is that well-known and most grisly and hideous of all ghost stores, the tale of the soldier in Petronius Arbiter. Now the belief in the '*Lupus-homen*' is very prevalent in parts of Northern Portugal ... nowhere is this belief invested with so many peculiar and gloomy circumstances as in Portugal."

Gypsy Wolf-Woman

The case of a werewolf referred to as a *ruvanush* (or "wolf-man") was related by Dr. Heinrich von Wlislocki in the July, 1891 *Journal of the Gypsy Lore Society.*

In 1881, the Gypsy fiddler Kropan and his wife existed by begging. They barely had enough money for food. But the wife seemed to have a remedy for the situation.

At night, the wife would sneak out of the house. One morning Kropan remained awake, awaiting the return of his woman. To his surprise his wife did not return, at least in the shape he had known her. A large gray wolf came into the bedroom with a dead lamb in its jaws. Within moments his wife was roasting the kill.

Kropan viewed the matter practically. Here was an easy method for getting meat, despite the fact that his wife was somewhat inhuman. The woman continued to kill animals while Kropan sold the excess meat in the neighboring villages. For a while, anyway, Kropan prospered.

Eventually Kropan's wife became too greedy, and the enormous wolf that ravaged the surrounding areas brought suspicion to the two Gypsies. The priest of the village knew her to be a *ruvanush* and proceeded to exorcise her and Kropan. Both Gypsies were bound helplessly by the villagers as the priest approached with his holy water. The woman screamed in agony as the water touched her flesh and a few moments later vanished. Kropan was then killed by the irate villagers.

Black Blood

The belief that black blood flows through the werewolf's veins persisted in Sicily. According to some writers, a man could be freed of his werewolf affliction if forced to suffer the shedding of this pitchcolored liquid.

Two such cases are supposed to have taken place in Palermo in 1889.

A wealthy nobleman in Palermo (or Sapaparuta, according to some writers) dreaded the rising of the full moon. For when that ominous sphere rose into the heavens, his face transformed to resemble that of a fanged wolf, and he was unable to suppress his lupine cravings.

Only one servant could be trusted with the dreaded secret of the werewolf. When the moon overcame his master, the servant let him loose to stalk the piazza of the city.

The household and the entire populace of the city were concerned with the matter. But no one could identify the werewolf.

One midnight, the werewolf was prowling through the streets and encountered a person who was not afraid of him. A soldier boldly faced the monster, drew his sword, and cut twice into its forehead, releasing a flow of black blood. Moaning from the pain, the werewolf collapsed at the soldier's feet. Everyone who came upon the scene was horrified to see that the fiend had resumed the features of the nobleman they all knew.

The nobleman did not die, but was happy that the shedding of his blood had removed the curse of the werewolf.

The second case involved a religious woman of Palermo. She regularly said her devotions. Apparently the prayers of this famous woman were not potent enough, for beneath her window one night appeared a snarling beast that sounded like a wolf.

Although she was terrified, the woman managed to peer through the curtains to see what manner of creature made such savage growls. The monster was man-like, yet resembled a large wolf. It gaped up at her hungrily, and then began to climb the wall. The gleaming fangs, licked by a wet tongue, were coming closer.

Instinctively she grabbed a poniard, said a prayer to Mary and St. Rosalie, and waited as the werewolf leaped onto her balcony. Foam spewed from its mouth as if from a rabid dog. It eyed her for what she would become — its next meal — unless she acted immediately.

She was not an especially strong woman, but her fear was sufficient to tax all of her strength. Ramming the poniard into the werewolf's forehead, she saw the ebony blood pour from the wound.

Groaning from the agony of the wound, the werewolf escaped into the night.

In the morning a Prince rewarded the woman with many precious gifts, her reward for shedding his blood and releasing him from his werewolf affliction.

ABBOT GILBERT
AND THE WEREWOLF

The Abbot Gilbert was returning to the Arc Monastery on the banks of the Loire River. He had been to a village fair and was weary from the wine and the hot sun. So weary was he in fact, that, while riding through the forest, he fell asleep and toppled from his horse.

He was not severely bruised, but had enough cuts in his flesh to attract a group of wild cats. Gilbert thought that he would soon perish at their fangs, when suddenly a werewolf appeared on the scene. The werewolf leapt valiantly into the assemblage of cats, and after a savage battle, emerged victorious.

Of course, Gilbert was not the sort of man tolerate someone so different as a werewolf. But even though Gilbert told him to go scampering off into the woods, the creature accompanied him back to the Arc Monastery. The Abbot told the monks what had happened. To his surprise, they welcomed the brute and dressed its wounds.

When dawn arrived, the werewolf regained his normal shape. Everyone was shocked to learn that, in truth, the monster was one of the clergy whose office was higher than Gilbert's. He scolded Gilbert for his actions in the forest, stripped him of half his rank, and inflicted a severe penance on him.

Shamed over the ordeal, Gilbert soon resigned voluntarily from his position.

IVAN BARANOFF

Tina Perovsky had virtually no reason to resent her marriage to Ivan Baranoff. He was a handsome man of considerable wealth and as chivalrous as a knight of old. There was one fault about him, however, that Tina could not tolerate. Ivan Baranoff occasionally transformed into a wolf.

Ivan and Tina had met at a party in Moscow sometime before the Revolution. They fell in love almost immediately and were married shortly thereafter. Being a wealthy widow, Tina was a worthy wife for Ivan.

Perhaps Tina should have noticed right from the beginning that Ivan was somewhat "different." Certainly he had some of the classic features of the werewolf. His eyes were cruel, almost wolfish, and his eyebrows met over the nose. The children from Tina's other marriage were terrified of him, as were her dogs, which barked whenever he came near them. These simper minds seemed to detect things about the man that Tina was too in love to see.

Despite the children's animosity toward him, Ivan continued to lavish them with presents and enough food to fatten them up. Then he made preparations to take the family away from Moscow and to his home in Omsk in western Siberia. Being a loving wife, Tina complied and brought the children along.

A feeling of ominous despair overcame Tina, however, as they passed through the foreboding forest in Omsk, with its countless gnarled trees, and eventually arrived at Ivan's villa. It was a terribly depressing building, smelling of animals, dark and barren with a floodplain. It was a house that could only have been designed by a crazed architect. The servants seemed suited to the place, for they prowled about the building like stalking animals.

Once in this home, Ivan managed to forget the manners that made such an impression on Tina in Moscow. He ate nothing but meat that was barley cooked. His manners were like those of a hungry wolf. And he delighted in letting the blood drip from his mouth.

One night Tina awoke to see Ivan silently creep out of bed. She followed him as he donned a coat of gray fur and exited by the window. Resolving at least the answer to the mystery of her husband, Tina watched him from the window, shivering as the cold wind blew in from the Tundra. When Ivan returned to bed, Tina pretended that she was asleep. But she managed to get a look at the blood on his face and hands.

In the morning Tina learned that a wolf had killed and devoured one of her dogs. For the next four nights Ivan continued to sneak out of the house, and the following morning another dog was found in the same condition as the others. She knew it must have been sheer coincidence but could not escape the feeling that was was Ivan who had killed the dogs in the manner of a wolf.

With the dogs dead, Tina had more reason to worry. For now, Ivan and the servants were looking rather hungrily at the children.

When Ivan left a note one morning, saying he was called away on business, Tina was relieved but even more terrified. Now she and the children were left to the mercies of the servants who gaped at her as wolves would an intended victim.

In order to get away from the servants, Tina went to the library, where she eventually fell asleep. She awoke at the strange sounds coming from the adjoining passageway. Peeking through the slightly open door, she saw an incredible sight. Prowling through the corridor was a werewolf — with a humanly shaped body but the head and claws of a wolf. Tina watched the monster as it was joined by two more werewolves. Then all three creept down the passageway. Horror seized her as she immediately thought of the children lying helplessly in their bedroom. She followed the creatures and found her worst fears actualized. The werewolves were bound for the childrens' room.

Before the werewolves entered the room, they saw Tina hiding among the shadows. Growling, one beast-man sprang for her throat, but she managed to escape into another room and slam the door.

Tina was momentarily safe, but her children were now exposed to the ravages of the werewolves. She could hear their screams mingled with the sounds of violence as the monsters attacked. Then one of the creature's heavy body slammed repeatedly at her door. An open window provided her with an escape. Climbing out into the cold night, Tina fled to the village with a horrible story to tell.

In the village, Tina learned that Ivan Baranoff and his servants had always been suspected werewolves. Father Rappaport, one of the men who listened to her story, believed it. He said that exorcism might drive out the demon responsible for the transformations from humans to beasts. He would perform the exorcism himself. With Colonel Majendie and twenty armed Cossacks accompanying him, the priest set out for the Baranoff property.

When the band neared Ivan's house, they were surprised by three man-like forms that leaped from the bushes. The werewolves fought their best but could not defeat twenty well-trained Cossacks. Within a short time the wolf-men were subdued and bound with ropes.

Father Rappaport was now able to prove the power of his exorcism. His method was according to old rituals. First he drew a circle with yellow chalk around the werewolves. Within the circle he drew another containing a small triangle and inscribed cabbalistic symbols. Oil lamps were placed on the outer circle and a miniature altar was erected on the inner circle. In an iron pot, hanging overhead, he mixed a weird concoction of ammonia, castoreum, sulfur, camphor, opium, hypericum, asafoetifa, and such additional ingredients as two live toads, a living snake, some mandrake and a fungus. As the clergyman ordered the demons out of the werewolves in the name of the Virgin Mary, he lashed the creatures with a whip made from birch, ash, and poplar branches.

As the priest did this, the werewolves became wildly uncontrollable and leaped into the forest. Colonel Majendie and his men hurried in pursuit of the monsters. It was nearly morning when the weary Cossacks finally tracked the werewolves to a cave, shot them to death and there saw them change back into men. There was nothing more to fear of the werewolves.

But the ground on which the Baranoff estate had been built remained haunted by the spirits of the werewolves and other phantoms.

REVENGE OF THE WERE-JAGUARS

Van Hielen, a Dutch trader, was visiting an Indian settlement on business when, at the edge of a dark forest, he heard a commotion. A boy of approximately seven years of age ran from the house, pursued by a heavyset woman who caught and beat him with a knotted club. Then she beat the boy's sister who was about three years older. When Van Hielen intervened and implored her to stop, the woman said that the boy and his sister Yarakna were evil and deserved to be punished. They had been bewitched by the evil eye of Guska, a hag killed with arrows in the market place the previous year.

Alone with the children, Van Hielen heard Yarakna say strange words. The Spirit of the Woods, and not the heavyset woman, was their mother, she confessed. Furthermore they would never again suffer because of the woman. The spirit would see to that.

That night Van Hielen spied upon the children and saw them creep from their hut and crawl on hands and knees along a forest path. He followed them, moving through the thick foliage. The area was alive with lurking death and Van Hielen was almost killed when he accidentally stumbled over a snake that attacked but missed.

Then he saw Yarakna and her brother, terribly ominous in their supposed innocence. They held hands and began to chant a weird incantation. Each taking an armful of flowers, the children dropped them reverently onto the leaves of a giant Victoria Regia water lily that floated on the brook. An ominous silence followed, making Van Hielen tremble.

Van Hielen could not believe that what he perceived was real. The objects of the forest were moving, twirling, dancing madly. The patch of earth before which Yarakna and her brother knelt apparently began to turn, then reversed to spin like a pyramid on its apex. The spinning thing vanished, to be replaced by a bulge in the earth that rose to seven or eight feet in height. Fearing for the children, he looked at them and saw only two greenish-yellow spheres, spinning and nearing him. At last all returned to normal except for the children, Where they had been were now a male and female jaguar, approaching him with obvious intentions.

At first, the two beasts seemed ready to attack. The female thrust her magnificent head into his face, then surprisingly led the other jaguar away from their cowering victim.

Thankful that he had been spared, Van Hielen hurried back to the village, A particular sense of foreboding drove him to the hut of the old woman who had beaten the children. A makeshift door had been crudely placed over the entrance of the hut. Something was wrong and he had a morbid dread of the nature of that *something*.

Van Hielen stepped up to the hut and what he heard sickened him. A large animal was crunching through what could only be bone. He knocked at the door but received no answer other than the crunching. At last the noises stopped and he reluctantly opened the door, seeing the half-devoured corpses of the woman strewn across the room. Two jaguars sprang from the corner, their mouths dripping blood. Instinctively Van Hielen raised his rifle but could not fire. For running toward him now were the bloody and wild-eyed forms of Yarakna and her brother.

THE DIRTY
OLD WEREWOLF

Just before the turn of the Twentieth Century, a werewolf prowled the Northumberland County area of Pennsylvania. People in the vicinity suspected a certain old man of being the lycanthropic monster. And so they scorned and avoided him.

The old man, however, was attracted to a twelve-year-old girl named May Paul. May busied herself with tending her father's sheep. While she worked, the strange old man would sit on a log, saying nothing, and just leer at her.

Naturally, May's parents did not like the idea of an old man watching their daughter day after day — especially an old man whom everyone said was a werewolf. But there was nothing that they could do since he had not technically done anything wrong. No one had proof that he was, in fact, a werewolf.

This situation persisted for years.

The full moon shone brightly one night when a hunter spotted a skinny wolf of considerable years walking across the road. There was a bounty of twenty-five dollars on the brutes and the hunter was determined to collect it. Raising his rifle, he fired a bullet into the wolf. The beast howled then took refuge in the bushes. Rather than pursue the wounded animal in the darkness, the hunter waited until morning when he made startling discovery.

There was no wolf carcass lying where it should have been.

Instead, killed by a bullet through the heart, was the old man rumored to be a werewolf. Now the man's condition seemed not to be just a rumor.

The old man was buried where he was found.

For the next twenty years May Paul tended sheep, never once being bothered by the hungry wolves that attacked the sheep of neighboring flocks. She claimed that she was still visited by the old werewolf who apparently watched over her own sheep.

The grave of the old man is still called *Die Woolf man's grob.*

The grave of the werewolf.

A Poisonous Werewolf

The werewolf of Finland has the property of possessing claws, which can scrape the skin and inflict a deadly poison into its victim's bloodstream.

Savanich and his son Peter were gathering wild strawberries when they heard the foreboding sound of a wolf. It was a time of the year when wolves were especially hungry. The cattle were not yet grazing in the fields and the wolves would attack the first human being they smelled.

Even as they spoke, Caspan, their sheepdog, rushed into the bushes to find a large gray wolf threatening its masters. A violent fight ensued between the two canines. Caspan's jaws locked upon the hairy neck of the brute and held it down helplessly.

While the wolf was so disposed, Savanich came forward with his knife and stabbed away until the beast transformed into an ugly old woman. She was not quite dead. Her hand was moving slowly toward Peter with its sharp forefinger.

Savanich called out to his son, but it was too late. The poisonous fingernail of the hag had already scratched his ankle. The woman smiled cruelly and then died.

Worried over the fate of his son, Savanich immediately took him home. Before they reached the door, Peter died.

THE WEREWOLF BURGOMASTER

A young man named Van Renner was proceeding to a shooting match of bows and arrows somewhere in the Netherlands. His journey was interrupted by the sounds of a young woman's screams.

With his bow and arrow gripped tightly, Van Renner hurried to the rescue, leaping over a dike and a low wall. He came upon the scene of a large gray wolf about to attack a beautiful girl.

Quickly he fired an arrow into the wolf, which fled for its life howling from pain.

Because both Van Renner and the girl were already married, there was no possibility of a romance springing from his valiant rescue. There was nothing more to do than bid each other farewell.

That evening after Van Renner returned home, he was summoned by his old friend the Burgomaster. Upon visiting the Burgomaster, the young man found him in bed, dying of a wound in his side.

The Burgomaster confessed that he could not die until he revealed to someone that werewolfery was hereditary in his family. It was he, in the shape of the wolf, who had received Van Renner's arrow. He wished to die knowing that he was leaving at least one friend, even though that friend was the cause of his demise.

Van Renner was so startled that he could not utter a single word. He could only watch the Burgomaster die.

THE WEREWOLVES AND THE DIAMONDS

A beautiful and arrogant woman named Madame Mildau was the society darling of Innsbruck. She was the star of all the finest parties. People would always gape at her beauty and the expensive clothes and jewels that she wore.

Madame Mildau was married to an overweight and much older man. While, for the most part, she despised him, she delighted in bending him to her will, especially when she wanted something. Unless he bought her a diamond tiara she'd fancied for a long time, she threatened to leave him. Mr. Mildau, though he could not afford the tiara, purchased it.

Madame Mildau, escorted by her obedient husband, attended one of the main balls of the year. He advised her not to wear the tiara because of a number of recent highway jewelry robberies. For once she obeyed her husband.

But Madame Mildau could not endure obeying him for long. She complained of a headache and asked her husband to take her home. Mr. Mildau complied with her wishes and was rewarded when they got home with a drugged drink. He would be asleep for hours and never saw his wife don her most expensive garments as well as the diamond tiara.

Although she was again the focal point of the ball, Madame Mildau began to worry. There were many consequences with which to reckon if her husband learned of her deceit. She decided to return home before he came out of his drugged state.

Madame Mildau was shocked to find a man emerge from the shadows of the coach in which she was riding home. He was as arrogant as herself, saying that there was nothing she could do to remove him. Even the driver was his own.

Immediately she clutched at her diamonds, believing the man to be one of the highwaymen about which she had often heard. He smiled, saying that, although he admired her jewels, they were not what he desired. When she demanded to know what he was, the young man said that, for the present, he was a man.

Madame Mildau did not understand his words, assuming to be in the presence of a madman. He questioned her about her husband and became curiously interested when she said that he was excessively fat. She shivered when he inquired if her husband was also tender.

The coach stopped. They were in the Wood of Arlen, one of the wildest and most remote areas of the Tyrol. The young man then said that he was a werewolf, as was his driver. Both would transform into monsters within an hour. And both were hungry.

Knowing that unless she did something fast, she would be a meal for two werewolves, Madame Mildau tried to explain how tough her flesh was. The young stranger had a better idea. He agreed to spare her life if she would give them the key to her house and allow them to devour her husband. With no reluctance, Madame Mildau agreed.

The driver took them to the Mildau house. There he securely bound

Madame Mildau, then entered the house with the other man. Mr. Mildau was still in his drugged condition and did not resist as he was carried outside. After the two fiends returned to the coach with their rotund prize, the young man released the woman from her bonds and then told her to drive the coach into the night unless she wanted to be served as dessert.

Madame Mildau cracked the whip and the coach began to roll. As the horses increased their speed she could hear, from the coach, the howling of wolves and the final screams of her husband.

The dawn was approaching, however, and she felt relieved. For Madame Mildau still had her diamonds.

WOLF-MAN
OF MONTENEGRO

About 1900, a Dr. Broniervski was on a geological expedition in Montenegro. His escort, Dugald Dalghetty, had been injured in an accident and was unable to accompany him on the expedition. Broniervski needed another guide and selected a Montenegrin named Kniaz, despite Dalghetty's warnings that he possessed the "evil eye."

Kniaz was an average-looking man, except for a peculiar look about his eyes. Some of the villagers seemed to regard the man with scorn, but that did not change Broniervski's mind. He noticed how his guide's lips twitched, how he muttered, and how his eyes shifted at the slightest sounds. There was nothing more to do, for Kniaz had already led the expedition into a forbidding area of rocks and forest which he described as the "land of the spirits."

The full moon shone brightly when the expedition stopped before what Kniaz called "the haunted valley." Piled like the fortifications of an ancient city, were rocks that gave the place an ominous appearance. A winding stream flowed snake-like between the rocks. Perhaps the valley was indeed haunted. The horses certainly sensed something out of the ordinary, for they would not take a step in that direction.

The valley was, Kniaz said, always under the spell of the gray spirits, and half man and half animal creatures, capable of transforming human beings into beasts.

After considerable coaxing, the horses were made to enter the valley. Kniaz, stating that he was too tired to go on, begged that they make camp for the night. During the night, however, the guide sneaked away.

Broniervski hurried to the stream and the rocks, noticing how the water flowed silently and how cold it was to his touch. But that was only the beginning of his strange encounter with the unknown.

A figure with the body of a man and the head of a wolf was kneeling at the stream. Broniervski could see the monster's moonlit hands gradually change into hairy claws. He was witnessing the transformation of a werewolf!

Noticing the intruder, the werewolf sprang at Broniervski, its eyes burning, its fangs aimed for his throat. Grasping him with its powerful grip, the beast-man hurled its victim to the ground. Blackness overcame Broniervski, as he believed a grisly death would follow.

When Broniervski regained consciousness, Dalghetty was seated on a rock. Beside him was he bloody corpse of Kniaz.

Dalghetty explained that he had been perturbed by the evil eye of the guide Kniaz. And so he followed him to this very spot where he managed to fire his rifle at the werewolf before the monster could sink its fangs into Broniervski's flesh. Now dead, the wolf-man metamorphosed back into its true form — Kniaz.

Dalghetty further explained to his startled listener that Kniaz had a grudge against a young farmer who had taken his girlfriend from him. In order to achieve a savage revenge, Kniaz drank the water of the enchanted stream, which changed him from a man into a semi-human beast.

THE KANDH WERE-TIGER

A man identified only as "Mr. K" had a terrifying experience with a were-tiger in the Kandh nation of Orissa. He had heard that the transformations from man into tiger took place in a certain spot in the jungle. Going to that place in order to prove or disprove the stories of tiger-men, Mr. K found a clearing surrounded by trees. Taking concealment amid the lush foliage of the jungle, he awaited the were-tiger.

At first he was almost disappointed. The person who came to the spot was a young boy, hardly the type that would transform into a savage cat. At first the boy seemed to act according to his age. But as he reached the clearing he took on a very serious and humble behavior.

The boy knelt before a staggering kulpa-tree and began to chant a strange prayer. To Mr. K., the night sky seemed to darken so that not a single star shone. The birds stopped singing and the entire area was engulfed in a strange stillness.

Terrified and thinking it would have been better to be somewhere else, Mr. K was nonetheless unable to take his eyes from the scene. The boy and the kulpa-tree gradually became more hazy to his eyes. As he watched, he heard a cry sounding both human and animal.

Then Mr. K saw a column of red light approach the native, who seemed to welcome it. Dropping to the ground., the boy wrote something in the dirt, placed a string of beads over the inscription, and began to speak an incantation. As he did this the light shot at the beads, causing them to blaze red.

The native put the necklace around his neck, clapped his hands together, and began to imitate the growls and snarls of a jungle beast. Mr. K kept observing the strange ritual and could swear that, as the actions of the boy became more bestial, he actually transformed into a tiger.

Immediately realizing that he had seen enough, Mr. K fled. Apparently the tiger had decided that the man had seen too much and raced after him, its jaws open for a meal of human flesh. The beast obviously possessed more than average intelligence. It could easily have overtaken Mr. K, but allowed him to make good his flight through the jungle.

A kulpa-tree stood before Mr. K and, even though receiving a gash on his cheek from the monster's claw, he managed to climb to safety. Eventually the were-tiger left him alone and went off, presumably in search of other game.

When Mr. K returned to the village he learned how a family, all of whom were enemies of the native boy, were found in their hut torn to pieces, as if by a tiger.

Relating what had happened to one of the natives, Mr. K was informed that it was the kulpa-tree that saved him from the were-tiger. The tree had religious significance and touching it made a man safe from the attack of any animal. The names of the gods Ram and Seeter were supposedly inscribed on the trees.

Before he left the area inhabited by the natives and the tiger-man, Mr. K. visited the tree that had supposedly saved him. He found the Sanskrit inscription on the tree and insisted, later, that it appeared as though written by a supernatural hand.

A Werewolf Attacks by Jans Weiditz, 1526.

THE FARMER AND THE WEREWOLVES

Claude Seignolle related the following werewolf case dated approximately 1900 in France.

A farmer had been going about his routine work when he spotted two wolves. Taking advantage of the fact that the brutes had not seen him, the farmer climbed a tree. From this vantage point he was able to observe the wolves.

Watching and listening, the farmer deduced that these were not ordinary wolves, but werewolves. They began to speak to each other in human voices. Finally one of them used a snuffbox and gave it to the other creature.

Dropping the snuffbox, the werewolves departed. When the farmer climbed down from the tree, he anxiously grabbed the snuffbox and tracked down its owner. Although the farmer knew the identity of one of the werewolves, he took the information to the grave in 1927.

One of the two werewolves died some years later of natural causes. Then a peculiar thing happened. Every morning there was discovered on his tombstone scratch marks — scratches dug into the stone by the claws of a wolf.

GHOST OF THE WEREWOLF

The case of a spectral werewolf was reported as having taken place in Estonia on the Baltic shores, in the early part of the 20th century.

Stanislaus and Anno D'Adhemar had been invited to stay a few weeks in the country home of a certain Baron and Baroness.

It was evening when the coach bearing Stanislaus and Anno was drawn through the woods by a pair of magnificent horses. Soon they were in a vast pine forest, rumbling over the rugged terrain. They were obviously in a place quite alien to a pair of big city dwellers. Birds they had never before encountered sang strange songs. But an unknown bird proved to be the least of their concerns.

Footsteps that could be made either by a human being or an animal were heard from behind. Someone or something was following the coach. The steps were so loud that, whatever the identity of the pursuer, it had to be large. The driver shuddered for it sounded to him like an extremely big wolf but running with the stride of a man.

To heighten the driver's fears, a wolf began to howl through the night.

Asking what was the matter, Stanislaus and Auno quivered as they heard the driver shout, "Wolves!" At the command of his two passengers, the coachman drove faster. His horses were running at their maximum speed, but still the footsteps of the unseen creatures were getting louder.

The creature was finally seen, approaching the coach with tremendous steps. It was naked, gigantic, and glowing, a hairy man-like form with a head resembling both that of a man and a wolf. The complexion of the monster was white and the eyes green.

Stanislaus and Anno were in complete terror. The monster was running alongside of the coach and might lash out at them with its claws at any moment. Suddenly the coach swerved in the skilled hands of the driver, drawing them all away from the ghastly apparition. When next time the looked into the forest the creature was nowhere to be seen.

They were thankful to reach the Baron's home unmolested. After they had narrated the strange event to the Baron, he revealed to them that the road they had taken had taken had long been haunted by the ghost of a werewolf killed there many years before.

WEREWOLVES AND THE MOUNTAIN ASH

In the early 20th century, in the Ardennes in Belgium, a young man named Bernard Vernand encountered three men, all of whom had characteristics of a werewolf when in human form. Their eyebrows met over their noses and Bernard's dog barked and acted as though terrified of them.

Despite his quick pace, Bernard noticed that the three men were trying to keep up with him. When he had walked to a dark spot in the road, where the trees were especially close to one another, he no longer heard the footsteps of the men. The dog suddenly ran away and Bernard, trusting in the senses of his pet, fled after him.

As he ran, he heard the sounds of whining canines and running feet, approaching him from behind. He ran as fast as his legs permitted but the footsteps grew louder. He was obviously being pursued by several animals, the species of which he shuddered to contemplate.

Bernard remembered stories that the ash tree was capable of warding off various types of demons. Climbing up the trunk of a mountain ash, he prayed that the tree would also have powers over the things that were running after him. He peered down from his vantage point to see a trio of werewolves halt abruptly at the foot of the trunk, snarl angrily, then bound away.

A young man returning to Waterloo from Quatre Bras saved himself from three werewolves by a similar act. He jumped into a ryefield, which had the same effect as the ash tree.

WEREWOLVES
OF MERIONETHSHIRE

Werewolves have often been reported in the Merionethshire area of the British Isles. But unlike the usual varieties of werewolf, these monsters appeared in the form of phantoms.

An incident involving such a special werewolf was told by J. Wentworth Day in July 9, 1932 edition of *The Passing Show*.

During the late 1880s, an Oxford professor and his wife were entertaining a guest in their small rented cottage in Merionethshire. The husband, while wading in the lake the day before, had discovered what appeared to be the skull of a large canine. The skull was placed on a kitchen shelf before the professor and his guest left the woman alone in the house.

It was evening and the woman had no desires to be left alone with the skull. Her apprehension was intensified when she heard something scratching at the kitchen door. The noise sounded as though it could have been a dog and she thought it best to immediately lock the kitchen door. However, as she entered the kitchen she saw, gaping at her through the window, a man-like abomination with a shaggy body and the face of a red-eyed werewolf. The monster was trying to get inside the house!

Luckily, her husband and his friend returned shortly. She told them her story and the two men resolved to wait for another appearance of the werewolf — this time with a loaded gun and some clubs.

After several hours, there came the sound of paws scratching on the kitchen window. Grabbing their weapons, the men saw the hideous werewolf glaring at them with blazing orbs. Instantly they rushed in pursuit of the beast, but its speed was too great. Already, the creature was running toward the lake where it presently vanished, never once disturbing the stillness of the water.

In the morning the professor returned the skull where he had found it and the spectral monster never reappeared.

Elliott O'Donnell related a similar case which also took place at Merionethshire.

A Miss St. Denis, an artist, had gone to paint and sketch the countryside of the British Isles one afternoon during the early 1900s. Miss St. Denis liked working from the railroad station, which provided her with a good view of the area and which was usually empty. In such an atmosphere, she could work efficiently and undisturbed.

But on that particular afternoon ,she noticed someone staring at her. The spectator was not the station master but a stranger, sitting on a small truck down the platform. Night was already approaching and the emptiness of the station made her even more uneasy.

Miss St. Denis coughed self-consciously. Then, to break the terrible, lingering silence, she asked the man if he could tell her the time. The man remained silent.

The sky was getting darker as Miss St. Denis grabbed her belongings together and started to walk away from the station. The only thing on her mind now was getting away from the stranger. There was no one in the vicinity to help her, should help be needed.

To her apprehension, the man was now following her and narrowing the gap between them with every step.

She increased her pace, aware that the farther she went in that direction the farther she would be from anyone else. Before her were the cliffs where, doubtlessly, no one would hear her if she screamed. Aware that she would be screaming shortly unless she took the initiative, she spun around to confront her pursuer.

What she saw was horrifying!

The man-like creature that was approaching her through the darkness had the head of a wolf. The head was covered with shaggy, gray fur and it opened its mouth to display its elongated white fangs. Crouching, its blazing eyes trained upon her, the werewolf made ready to spring.

Having no weapons, she quickly reached into her pocket and removed a flashlight. Clicking it on, she trained the beam into the werewolf's face.

The monster then did something which made Miss St. Denis gape with disbelief. As the beam struck the monster's face, the beast stopped to shield itself from the light. Within another few moments the werewolf of Merionethshire literally vanished.

The Phantom Werewolf
and the Geologists

Elliott O'Donnell included a first person account in *Werewolves* which seems to be a different version of that involving the Oxford professor and the werewolf skull discovered at Merionethshire.

Two amateur geologists, a Scotsman and his English grandson, were looking for fossils in caves and quarries somewhere in the British Isles. What they uncovered was more startling than the unearthing of the remains of any prehistoric animal.

In the bed of what had once been a lake, the geologists uncovered a strange skeleton. The bones seemed to be those of a human, yet the skull was that of a wolf. The only such hybrid of a man and wolf was a werewolf and the old man thought he had a priceless addition to his fossil collection. The area was once a haven for werewolves, he told his grandson, and they were lucky to make such a rare find.

The skeleton was carted off to the house for further study.

Naturally, one does not have the bones of a werewolf in the kitchen without something bizarre happening.

The grandson was home alone that night. He was reading to distract his thoughts from the hideous thing in the kitchen. But as he read he heard an ominous sound coming from that room. Something was rapping on the kitchen window as though it wanted entrance to the house.

Quickly he went into the kitchen and gaped with horror at the creature just outside the window. It stood upright like a man, but the face and claws were those of a wolf. The werewolf's ghost, he thought, was returning from the world of the dead to reclaim its stolen bones.

As the monster lifted an arm, apparently to smash through the glass, the young man ran from the kitchen and awaited the inevitable encounter with the brute. To his astonishment, the werewolf did not break the glass. Nor did it make another appearance. When the rest of the family returned, he told them what had happened. The werewolf was nowhere to be seen and everyone smiled over his wild imagination.

Perhaps it was only his imagination, stimulated by the fear of being alone in the house with such a monstrosity as a werewolf's skeleton. Just as a precaution, however, the old man and his grandson returned the strange bones to the tarn from which they were taken.

Illustration by Fredrick Madden, Cambridge, 1832.

WEREWOLF FLOWER
OF TRANSYLVANIA

Various flowers are believed to have the property of transforming people into werewolves. One case involving such flora, reported about 1911,featured Ivan and Olga, the children of storekeeper Otto Kloska and his wife Vera. The event took place in the village of Kerovithc in the Transylvanian Alps, Romania.

Olga had suggested to her brother that they pass the time picking flowers. They would string the flowers together and whoever produced the best wreath would be the winner of their game. The children descended into a deep pit where many flowers were growing.

The girl was intrigued by a very white flower resembling a sunflower. It was pulpy and soft and had a somewhat sweet and sickening odor. She wanted to put it in her buttonhole.

Ivan, sensing something ominous about the plant, warned Olga against keeping it. Nevertheless, she placed the flower into her buttonhole and began to parade about pompously, like a high society woman wearing an expensive gown and corsage.

In keeping with her play-acting, Ivan was about to salute Olga as might an admiring soldier, when he noticed something strange about the girl. Protesting her advance, Ivan tried to climb out of the pit.

Vera Kloska hurried out of the house at the sounds of Ivan's screams. So frantic was the woman that she slipped over the edge of the pit and broke one of her legs. But she soon forgot her own pain. A wolf with gray fur was chewing on young Ivan and was about to rip into his throat with its fangs.

The only weapon the woman had was a long steel skewer that she used for attaching her washing line. She wanted to kill the wolf with the spear-like object, but Ivan warned her that this was really Olga, transformed into a wolf by the magic of the flower.

Vera had to make a decision — kill her daughter or sacrifice Ivan to satisfy the hunger of the werewolf. At last she decided that Ivan must live and drove the skewer through the werewolf's eye and into its brain. She wielded the skewer a second time, but accidentally struck her son.

When a villager later came upon the scene, Vera was already mad, laughing over the corpses of Olga and Ivan.

SANTA CLAUS AND THE WEREWOLF

After acquiring a sizable amount of money through an inheritance, a married couple named Anderson purchased some land in Cumberland in a remote area at the foot of the hills. The year was approximately 1911.

The howls of wolves were frequently heard and the Anderson's fearful servants, unable to endure the noises, left.

On one particular night, after the children had been put to bed, the couple heard a noise that sounded like a wolf below the window. Looking outside, Mr. Anderson saw only the full moon. The wolf sounds persisted, nevertheless, followed by the sound of the front door opening. From the stairs came the sound of footsteps, like those made by an animal. When Mr. Anderson went to investigate, however, he found nothing amiss.

The Andersons realized that they were enveloped in a mystery, one that could have terrifying consequences. Fighting a wolf that was made of flesh and blood was one matter; encountering an unseen creature that continued to growl so hauntingly was another.

It was nearly Christmas and Mr. Anderson was telling his children of the approaching visit of Santa Claus. The children did not believe in the old gentleman with the presents, and so their father decided to disguise himself as Santa and surprise them.

There was a full moon shining that Christmas Eve. Mr. Anderson, dressed as Santa Claus, and bearing a sackful of gifts over his shoulder, was a making his way to the children's room. He stopped halfway up the stairs, startled by the foreboding sound of a wolf yelping. But the yelping was strangely reminiscent of a human voice. Fearing that the beast was somewhere in the house, Mr. Anderson proceeded to the bedroom, opened the door, and crept inside, just as the clock sounded midnight.

But as "Santa Claus" entered the room, so did a hairy, shadowy man-like shape. One of the children threw a slipper, almost hitting Mr. Anderson. The other children awoke to see the two fantastic characters standing in their bedroom. They saw a petrified Santa Claus, gaping at a nude figure with the body of a man and the head of wolf, its fangs dripping and eyes blazing like points of fire.

Mrs. Anderson was, however, unaware of the horror that confronted her husband and children upstairs. Anxious to see how Mr. Anderson was doing, she ascended the stairs and entered the bedroom with a lit candle. As the light fell upon the monster, it mysteriously vanished. Immediately, as a precaution, the Andersons lit every candle in the house.

Mr. Anderson needed little deliberation to decide upon selling the house. Yet, before the new owners moved into the building, Mr. Anderson resolved to learn the truth behind the mysterious wolf. In a cave directly behind the house, he discovered a human skeleton missing the skull. Nearby was the skull of wolf. In order to prevent any further hauntings from the phantom, Mr. Anderson incinerated the bones. Evidently he did his job well, for there were no reports from the new owners of the house of the ghostly werewolf.

SAIYI, THE WERE-TIGER

The following account by C.P. Mills was published in 1922 under the tile "Were-Tigers of the Assam Hills":

"It should be understood that the wound on the human body does not appear simultaneously with that inflicted on the animal, but some days later, when the man has learnt of the condition of leopard or tigers. This point is illustrated by an incident which occurred in March, and of which I heard immediately afterwards.

"While Mr. Hutton was in camp at a village called Melomi, one of his Angami interpreters, while wandering round with a gun, met a large tiger. He fired and wounded the animal, hitting it rather far back. The beast got away, however. It was said, more in jest than in earnest, that the tiger was really a man-tiger. This came to the ears of Saiyi of Zumethi, a subordinate in the Civil Works Department, but a tiger-man withal. He announced to his friends that his tiger had been wounded, and took to his bed. Three days later he was met by Nihu, head interpreter of Kohima, being carried into Kohima on a stretcher for treatment in the Government hospital. Nihu, who is a most intelligent and entirely reliable man, told me that he questioned and examined Saiyi, who said that he was suffering terrible pains in the abdomen owing to the wound inflicted on his tiger, and showed an enflamed swelling on either side of the stomach, corresponding, of course, to the entrance and exit hole of the bullet which had hit the tiger. He eventually died in the Kohima hospital."

TEI, THE
WERE-PANTHER

William Seabrook's investigations into strange phenomena have included cases of lycanthropy. Not all of these cases have involved men transforming into wolves. The case of the panther-man of the Ivory Coast as well as similar instances, were published in his book, *Witchcraft: Its Power in the World Today.*

Tei had been petty chief of the Yafouba and was occasionally employed as a clerk in the administrative offices at Dakue. Now he sat in prison awaiting his execution. He was a known panther-man and sometimes the pet lycanthrope of the area. But he had been caught in the act of murdering his jungle love, Blito, a crime to which he admitted.

The murdered young woman had also been the love of Administrator Clouzet, which made for complications.

Witnesses had supposedly seen the panther-man after his act of violence. Tei himself suggested to the district officials that the murder was the work of a Liberian cult of leopard-men. Three Liberians were held as suspects in the crime. But when it was proven that they could not have done the terrible act, suspicion fell upon Tei himself.

All the articles attesting to Tei's guilt were found in his home — bloodstained gloves, a panther skin, plus all of Blito's bloody jewelry. The evidence was so incriminating that Tei readily confessed his guilt.

Seabrook visited Tei in the prison yard. The native confessed to his strange condition by which he assumed the shape and temperament of a jungle cat and relished in the transformation.

To accomplish this metamorphosis (which occurred at unpredictable times) Tei would first don the panther skin and gloves, and then rub himself with the fat of the animal and devour its liver. A wild dance would follow, with a final leap through the air completing the strange rite.

Naturally, Seabrook wondered why a man who changed into a real panther needed all those fetish trappings. To this Tei answered sincerely that he would like to be prepared if the change back to human form occurred at an inopportune moment. Tei took no chances.

Seabrook attributed the entire case to hallucination. Tei actually believed he had transformed into a panther. Moving swiftly through the shadows, he appeared as a blur of claws and fur to Blito and the numerous witnesses to the attack. When no real panther tracks were discovered, the witnesses naturally were on the lookout for a panther-man.

Most importantly, Tei really *believed* that he was transformed into an animal and acted accordingly.

The witnesses occasionally visited Tei in prison, saying that he was not responsible for what he did as a panther. They believed that the firing squad, to which he had been sentenced, would provide a final cure of his tragic ailment. They were also lingering around the prison to observe the transformation into a panther after his body was riddled with bullets. The firing squad did their duty. To the disappointment of many, the body of Tei remained human.

THE HYENA WORE EARRINGS

The case of the female hyena of Ouahigoya was also related by William Seabrook.

There was considerable concern over an animal shot by a young Englishman. He had been hunting lion at night, but shot something that caused him great worry. A dead hyena lay at his feet. Hyenas were often shot in that area and there was usually no reason for concern. This time, however, was a different matter. The hyena was a female and wore golden earrings, studded with jewels, in its pierced ears.

The Englishman was given a room at the administrative house while the hyena carcass was locked in the office.

The authorities, assuming that this was the result of some native superstition, called in the local chief, witch doctor, priests and other natives. Surprisingly, none of them had ever seen a hyena with earrings.

Administrator-General Bercole went to the Ouahigouya palace of the Yatanga Naba, Black Pope of the Mossi, in an attempt to clear up the mystery.

According to the Yatanga, Sarab'na was the youngest daughter of a native king called Sanou. During the princess' initiation as a woman, the witch doctors supposedly discovered, through their magic, that she was possessed by the spirit of a terrible hyena. At times, this animal soul would dominate her, forcing her to attack her parents as would a hungry animal. To destroy the girl would only release the hyena demon to inflict horror and death upon the land. The Yatanga then provided further details of the story.

Sarab'na was locked in a cellar below the temple and there subjected to numerous indignations at the hands of her sisters and the priests. Their intention was to make her body too uncomfortable for the hyena spirit, and either to drive it out or to force it into metamorphosing her body into animal form. They did their work well, at least insofar as torturing the girl, while the priests shrieked their incantations. But their work was not thorough enough, for there was no exorcism of the hyena soul or transformation.

Bercole and the Yatanga, however, felt there were more materialistic motives for what had been done to the girl. It was finally revealed that the sisters had bribed the Priests into saying she was really a demon. This was done out of jealousy. Sarab'na had been betrothed to a Songhai Prince and would soon, through their marriage, receive considerable wealth. Naturally, the Prince could not marry a woman possessed by a hyena!

Sanou, being gullible, believed that the tortured girl, who ate raw meat and crawled on all fours, was indeed a monster to be destroyed. His other daughters were crafty and played upon his gullibility. The hyena spirit, they said, would not come out so long as Sarab'na was in a confined location. The transformation would, however, take place if the girl were to be set free.

Among the cliffs, the demented girl was let loose. There her sisters murdered her and tossed her body to the crocodiles.

The crime might have gone unnoticed had not the priests decided to enhance their own prestige in the area. They trapped a female hyena, inserted the earrings into its ears, and set it free, hoping that it would be seen and killed by a superstitious native. Unfortunately for them it was a professional hunter who bagged the animal."

As a result, the murders were discovered, apprehended, and placed in charge of the Yatanga Naba, who dealt out his own justice.

White Panther-Woman of Africa

Seabrook also recorded the following case history, which stemmed from rumors that a white man had been holding an animal-woman captive in a cage in the Saraban. According to stories, the woman's mouth was frequently seen smeared with blood. And she enacted the role of a wild, captive panther.

Bercole, the Administrative-General, and Seabrook were among the group that made the perilous journey to the Saraban in order to learn the truth concerning the stories of this panther-woman.

The man who supposedly kept the woman in the cage was a planter named Joseph Hecht, a former citizen of Luxembourg and Marseille. When Hecht was questioned by Bercole about the rumors of the panther-woman, he admitted, to everyone's surprise, that the stores were true. The panther-woman in question was his wife, Marthe.

Even the witch doctors could not find a cure for Hecht's wife. According to the planter she would occasionally become possessed by the spirit of a beast as a result of a madness that she had contracted. On at least two occasions, when Marthe supposedly became a wild animal, she was found with blood smeared over her jaws.

Hecht related his wife's bizarre history to the men who had come to his plantation. Her terrible plight had begun, not in the superstition-ridden jungle, but rather in civilized France. After they were married and honeymooning in Marseille, Marthe became horrified of someone she had seen in the street. Terrified that she was being followed, she confessed that she had once been initiated into a weird mystic cult with origins rooted in medieval times. She had engaged in their strange rituals, including lying nude upon the altar and consuming the blood of animals. Often she would become possessed, at which times she would act like a wild beast.

Marriage to Hecht provided an escape for the poor woman. When Hecht learned of his wife's malady he listened to her plea to take her to some remote area of the world. He decided to make a new life for them both in Africa.

Marthe lived a normal life until she heard the rhythmic sounds of tom-toms from a native village. The natives were worshipping their demon gods with the usual dancing, chanting, and masks. Marthe joined their ceremony, began to act like a beast, and was identified as *G'nouna*, the female version of the forest's Great Demon *Gla*. When the woman proceeded to prowl through the jungle and the natives found her with a bloody mouth, they no longer regarded her as a goddess. Now she was a monster, *kai gaibou* ("like a panther"), and was possessed by the creature's soul.

The husband found that the most successful means of preventing his wife from becoming a menace during her "spells." was to keep her locked in the elaborate and comfortable cage he had added to the house.

Seabrook, Bercole, and the others approached the woman in the cage. At the time, she was in her normal state and smoking a cigarette. Obviously she resented the intrusion on her strange form of privacy.

Bercole asked her if he should bring charges against Hecht for having her thusly confined.

The woman in the cage said that she had no complaints and would do whatever her husband thought best.

Yi King and the Werewolf

Finally, Williams Seabrook related the following personal werewolf encounter in his book, *Witchcraft: Its Power in the World Today.*

Natasha Filipovna was a Russian refugee with exotic features, including white flashing teeth and a beautiful head of coarse brown hair. Her life had become entangled with various sensational events. The occult, a friendship with the notorious Rasputin, and crystal gazing (initiated by a Russian fortune-teller in Cleveland) had all become a part of her life experiences. While gazing into her crystal ball, she once saw herself as a Mongol woman using a primitive stone knife to cut meat from a dead bear. Fantacies of her reverting to the primitive became more frequent. And though she despised wearing animal skins and cave dwelling, she hated living in Cleveland even more.

In the summer of 1923 Seabrook's friend, Bannister, convinced Natasha to let him try an experiment with her involving the *Yi King* (or *I Ching*), the oldest work of magic and divination written in China. The experiment was to be conducted in Bannister's apartment-studio, which was adorned with masks, idols, and other magical paraphernalia.

The studio was in semidarkness. Natasha knelt in the center of the room, according to the instructions given her. Bannister and Seabrook both watched intently. She tossed the *ko* hexagram (which refers to hide, skin, fur, leather, and to the act of flaying and undergoing change or transformation). Entering a trance, Natasha saw the door of the hexagram open to her. Then she spoke incredible words relating how she was a white-furred creature lying in the moonlit snow. Her narrative climaxed with her imitating the yelps and pants and baying of a wolf.

Bannister was elated, as he believed he had just witnessed an actual case of regression to a previous animal existence. In the semi-darkness he actually believed that he saw Natasha's face undergo an actual physical transformation. But Seabrook assured him that the wolfish characteristics had always been there.

It was now time to bring Natasha out of the trance.

To the astonishment of Bannister and Seabrook, Natasha was still in her wolf condition. Instead of returning to normal, she snarled hungrily and then tried to rip out Bannister's throat with her teeth. It took both men to wrap the woman in blankets, subdue her, and bring her to full human awareness by placing ammonia under her nose.

A week later, Natasha revealed something which seemed to explain the basis of her dreams of becoming a wolf. As a child in Russia she had often seen the wolves bathing in moonlight and running through the snow. In an innocent way she desired to be like them, to be accepted into the pack and share in their freedom. Under the trance of the *Yi King*, Natasha Filipovna was able to have her wish fulfilled.

THE WEREWOLF PRANKSTER

A policeman of the town of Alsuce was tried for murder in November, in Uttunheim near Strasburg, 1925.

He was accused of killing a young boy. But the policeman claimed that what he shot was no human being at all — but a werewolf.

The policeman maintained that he had been haunted by beasts with the faces of men. These were not mere hallucinations, he insisted, wishing that they had been. No, he continued, the faces were those of the boy who had the magic power to change his form to that of the beast.

THE WERE-TIGER OF SLIM VALLEY

To the Malayan natives, the were-tiger is the indigenous lycanthropic monster. They can cite numerous cases of men being transformed into the great cats. Haji Abdallah, of Korinch in Sumatra, was caught naked in a tiger trap and fined for the number of buffaloes killed while he took on the shape of a beast. Tigers have emerged from bushes where men had gone to disrobe. Still other men have vomited feathers after taking on the shape of tigers and devouring fowl.

Sir Hugh Clifford included the following case history of a Malayan were-tiger in his book, *In Court and Kampong*, published in 1927.

A Korinchi trader named Haji Äli came into the Slim Valley with his sons Abdulrahman and Abas. After their trading was done, the three decided to stay in the area. As long as they were settling down, Haji Äli announced his desire for a wife.

Haji Äli selected a comely young woman named Patîmah. She was the daughter of poor peasants and was glad to marry a man of such wealth. She was about to embark on a new and prosperous life. And so she eagerly went through the wedding ceremony, enjoyed the feast afterwards, and accompanied her new husband to his home among the palm trees and fruit groves.

Her parents could see no reason for the subsequent strange behavior of the Patîmah. They found her shortly thereafter, pounding on their door, disheveled as though having gone through a terrible ordeal, and with a look of horror on her lovely face.

Patîmah's first days as a wife and housekeeper were trying. She cooked rice poorly, which made Abdulrahman and Abas grumble. Haji Äli would mysteriously leave the house every evening after the Usa or hour of evening prayer. On the third night of successive disappearances, Patîmah lay awake in her bed, wondering what had become of her husband. There was a sound outside the locked door and she believed it to have been made by Haji Äli. She shuddered at the sight of the terrible creature gaping at her from the top rung of the ladder leading to the threshold of the house.

The creature appeared to be an adult tiger but with a body similar in shape to that of a man. She wanted to scream, to run, but was unable to move. She was virtually paralyzed with fright. What followed made her horror even worse, for she saw the striped monster slowly re-form into the image of her husband. Regaining her senses, Patîmah leaped from the doorway and fled into the night. Although the jungle was a dangerous place for a young girl, she bolted through the thorns and creepers that were barely lit by the moonbeams. Anything was better than staying another moment in the house of the tiger-man.

The story of Haji Äli, the were-tiger, swiftly spread through the village. The man with whom everyone was once eager to trade was now earnestly avoided.

The were-tiger caused no more trouble in the area until the slaying of a handsome water buffalo belonging to the Headman, Penghflu Mat Saheh. The beast had been killed by a tiger, but thus far only the Headman knew this. Instead of spreading rumors that the were-tiger was again on the prowl, he constructed a special trap rigged with a spring-gun. The carcass of the water buffalo constituted the bait. If the carnivore became greedy and returned for its kill, the trap would kill or severely wound it with bolts and slugs shot from the gun.

The next night *something* was heard being caught in the trap. Not wanting to confront a wounded tiger at night, Penghflu Mat Saheh waited until the next morning before examining the killer of his water buffalo. Then, accompanied by a number of armed men from the village, he hastened to the trap. Surely a tiger had been there, for leading away from the trap was a trail of tiger tracks.

The tiger was wounded and easy to follow. The animal mostly walked on three legs, the fourth being injured by the trap. The trail of blood staining the grass made the search easier.

The pursuit of the tiger took the hunters up-stream and eventually to the bamboo fence of a native compound. They entered the gate and found the end of the tiger's bloody trail — the house of Haji Äli from which Patîmah had fled.

Abas received the visitors into his house. When Penghflu asked about the patch of blood on the floor, Abas said that the family had killed a goat. When asked to produce the skin of the supposedly slaughtered goat, Abas cleverly stated that the carcass had been thrown into the river.

Penghflu, however, was still not satisfied. He demanded to know the nature of Haji Äli's malady. The only answer he received was at swordpoint, when Äbdulrahman ordered them out of the house.

As the visitors descended the ladder, they passed an inner chamber where the ground was stained red and where Haji Äli's sickbed might have been. They never learned the answer, for his two sons had followed them out and locked the door, preventing their investigation.

No one ever learned more about the family of ex-traders, for they packed all their belongings and mysteriously fled the vicinity, abandoning all their crops to the birds and the elements. Some months later, it was noted that Haji Äli's right leg was lame, as though he might have caught it in a tiger trap.

CULT OF THE
LEOPARD-MEN

During the 1930s, the Belgian Congo was plagued by a particular variety of human animal. Victims were frequently found slain as if by leopards. (A leopard holds down its victim's shoulders and head with its claws while disemboweling the stomach, a particularly distinctive technique.) There seemed no doubting the existence of killer leopards that preferred human beings as victims and liked the taste of human flesh better than that of any animal.

But there were stories circulating that the fiendish killers were not really animals — but leopard-men.

The sometimes cannibalistic killings were actually the work of a large number of Anyoto tribesmen who were members of an African secret group called the Leopard Cult or Society of Leopard Men. The Leopard Cult has existed and been a problem for hundreds of years, and efforts made by the authorities have failed to eliminate it.

Although the leopard-men do not physically transform into carnivorous felines, they do mimic the behavior of leopards to the extent that the men seem to believe a metamorphosis has occurred.

The leopard man's desire to become the animal after which the cult was named is elaborate and, perhaps, even more terrible considering that there is no real transformation. He wears a leopard skin in order to resemble the great cat, while he prowls through the shadows of the jungle.

Such killers carry facsimile leopard claws, capable of mauling a victim before he can put up much resistance. In their frenzy, the leopard-men are sometimes bold enough attack victims in their homes, disemboweling them and even eating their flesh.

The leopard-men have assumed such behavior in order to take on the power and spirit of the impressive jungle beasts. Practically speaking, despite the lack of physical transformation, the members of the Leopard Cult *are* efficient lycanthropes.

Juba Kennerley endeavored to learn if there were any truths to the stores of physical transformations among Africa's Society of Leopard-Men. During his travels in Africa, he experienced many mysterious happenings. A witch doctor named Chusimbo exhibited a leopard that made sounds as though processing a human voice. Kennerley denied that the witch doctor was skilled in ventriloquism. In the jungle, two lycanthropes, growling like leopards, attacked and killed game with their teeth and nails. Venturing to Burmah, Kennerley recalled a man named Maung Taw who was speared to death because it was believed that he was a were-tiger who had previously raided his own camp. On a later date, a tiger was killed while Moung Po Yin, a man believed to be a were-tiger vanished forever.

In Australia, Kennerley made the acquaintance of a very intelligent dog that led him to a source of water. After striking the dog, he noticed a similar bruise which suddenly "appeared" on the face of his friend. This said Kennerley, may be an example of a man's spirit fusing with that of an animal.

In Canada, he encountered a man whose twin brother had died, supposedly after his spirit had entered the body of a moose. This animal was fatally wounded while engaged in a battle of the rutting season. The man's "spirit" then returned to his human body to die. The brother was arrested for fratricide. Also in Canada, Kennerley met a man named Chilkoot Tom who had stolen an Indian squaw. The squaw occasionally listened to the howling wolves as if they were calling her. One night Tom awoke to find the woman sitting on top of him, growling like a wolf and biting his throat with her teeth. Surrounding them was a pack of gray wolves. The squaw then blended in with the pack and led them into the night as through she belonged with them.

Many attacks by leopard-men occurred in Lagos in 1946, while a similar society of lion-men terrorized Tanganyika the following year. As late as the 1960s, men were found disemboweled and devoured — victims of the Leopard Cult.

DANCE OF THE WERE-JACKALS

Nandor Fodor recorded an account of were-jackals in the December, 1945 edition of the *Journal of American Folklore:*

"I have in my records a first hand account regarding lycanthropy. This account is dated March 23rd, 1933 and it comes from a Dr. Gerald Kirkland, then a 37 year-old medical practitioner at Trellwis, Glamorganshire, England and formerly Government Medical Officer in Southern Rhodesia.

"Dr. Kirkland had seen a native jackal dance and could almost swear to it that two natives actually transformed themselves into jackals. His account, first sent to me in a letter, was printed two years later; it is not only vivid and detailed, but exposes the psychological motive behind the lycanthropic ceremonial he witnessed. The motive is clearly orgiastic. Desiring to be as potent as only dogs can be, the African natives succeeded, after eating "high" meat and drinking large quantities of liquor, in playing the parts of jackals with uncanny realism. By the time the orgy reached its climax Dr. Kirkland was so overwrought that he may have easily entered into the psychic atmosphere of the group. The fact that he was unobserved (if he was) would not exempt him from such contagion.

"The phenomena he describes represent an evolutionary regression, an escape from the human onto the animal level. Eating ill-smelling meat and heavy drinking was apparently part of the self-persuasion necessary for the lycanthropic climax. Besides the purely sexual and sadistic motives, the cannibalistic and the necrophillic instinct may be divined behind the escape, because on the animal level no guilt is attached to satisfying them. The gateway to the outpour of the primitive unconscious was the *Nanga* or witch doctor in trance, who acted collectively for the group and whose normal office as witch doctor invested the ceremonial with the stamp of legitimacy."

The Lion-Man

The *pondoro* are lions believed to shelter the souls of deceased native chieftains. Such lions are regarded as sacred beasts, as are the cows of India.

When a lion was prowling about the carcass of a recently slain buffalo, a native reprimanded it for sinking to the lowly rank of scavenger. Why could not the *pondoro* use its hunting prowess to kill its own food, instead of gnawing on the meat intended for the native villagers? The native had lost all respect for the former chief.

An explorer present at the time reported that the *pondoro* was finally driven away by a piece of meat soaked in strychnine.

TWO MORE
RECENT WEREWOLF CASES

The werewolf tradition continues to endure despite the scientific sophistication of our modern world. Although scientists tell us that the transformation of man into animal is absurd and impossible, beliefs in werewolves are still strong.

There is the case of the farmer in Bourg-la Reine, France. The farmer was a known sorcerer in his land, with a house filled with all the bizarre equipment typically owned by a black magician. Wax dolls and amulets adorned the place and helped frighten away curiosity seekers.

In 1930, neighbors swore that the farmer assumed the physical shape of a wolf at night and enacted the role of that animal.

As late as 1946, a Navaho Indian reservation was seized in a grip of terror. A Native American werewolf was supposedly preying on a trading post on the reservation. The monster was not only blamed for killing sheep and cattle, but also opening graves and murdering human beings. He seemed especially to prefer slaying and devouring woman.

HOUSE OF
THE WEREWOLF

The following case history of a *loup-garou* was first related in the pages of *Fate* magazine by Farley James, and later reprinted in the book *Strange Fate.*

Farley James had rented a house in the Bel Air district of Cap Hatien in February, 1944. This was Haiti, a country steeped in traditions of zombies and werewolves.

The house of the *loup-garou* was situated some twenty yards to the right of James' house. The place was avoided by the Haitians and those who were forced to pass the building did so only after first making the Sign of the Cross. Fetius, James' chauffeur who was extremely knowledgeable in the traditions of Haiti, also crossed himself as he looked in the direction of the house and began to tell his employer of its strange occupant.

The house had belonged to an officer in the Garde de Haiti, a man of high society who also had the distinction of being a werewolf. This was no ordinary werewolf, however, but a monster surrounded by a green mist which allowed the beast to cover considerable areas of land. When the moon was full, the greenish *loup-garou* would seek out its favorite food — the blood of children.

The peasants resolved to destroy the beast-man themselves but were thwarted by the commanding colonel. This officer attempted to prevent the inevitable violence by giving the suspected werewolf a transfer to the garrison at Port au Prince.

The menace of the Cap Hatien werewolf had apparently ended, or so everyone thought, until a couple with a year-old child moved into the house. One night the child's screams awakened them both. The parents ran to the crib but to their horror found the child gone. The child was discovered outside the house. Except for two bleeding wounds on the neck, the child had not been harmed. And throughout the house wafted the fading odor of brimstone accompanied by a weird green glow.

The werewolf did not return for the child. But during the succeeding nights its greenish presence was seen outside through the windows.

Fetius summed up his narrative and cringed when James suggested tracking down the *loup-garou*.

Alone in the house, James was awakened from a deep sleep by the sound of *something* trying to push in the front door. Grasping a loaded .45, he opened the door, finding nothing where the unknown intruder should have been. He looked out toward the house of the *loup-garou* and saw the dreaded green light flickering through the windows. James felt a shudder throughout his body as he became aware of the distinct smell of brimstone.

Still clutching the pistol, James returned to his bed where he remained awake with the light burning. If the werewolf returned, James resolved that he would be ready for it.

The following afternoon James related his experience to some friends, all of whom expressed a desire to help him in his quest for the *loup-garau*.

They all sat upon the veranda that night, awaiting the rising of the full moon and their unearthly quarry. As if on schedule, the green light appeared from window to window in the house of the wolf-man. Armed with canes, a machete, and the .45, the group moved toward the otherwise dark structure. From different directions the small band stormed the house. When they ran inside they found the building to be empty and completely devoid of any light, green or otherwise.

The dust within the house was undisturbed. And everyone was certain that no one had left the house. Yet lingering about the place was the smell of brimstone. Something unexplainable was definitely taking place.

The group waited, hoping for a return of the *loup-garou*. Within the next two hours the green light and smell of brimstone made three appearances. Despite the band's best attempts to capture the elusive creature, the results were always the same as before. By midnight, the hunters gave up the quest and vacated the place.

The haunting by the mysterious werewolf did not, however, desist. James repeatedly saw that green light, smelled brimstone, and heard the thumping all about his house. At last, he concluded that the *loup-garou* was singling him out for its next victim. On a morning in April, Farley James waited for Fetius to chauffeur him, forever, from the house of the green-glowing werewolf.

TRIAL FOR A HIPPOPOTAMUS

A case of Lycanthropy, the type involving animal souls, was related by G. Jones in 1947.

A hippopotamus had caused considerable damage to a cabbage patch somewhere in Africa. The damage caused by such a beast could more than infuriate the owner of the cabbage patch. He took the matter to court and was given two pounds for what had been maliciously done to his property.

Maliciously, of course, implied that the damage was not solely the work of a dull-witted hippo.

His true enemy — the one *really* responsible for the damage — was allegedly a member of a secret society. A characteristic of the society was that the members also had animal souls.

The defendant made no attempt to deny that his own animal soul resided in the body of the hulking brute that had ruined the cabbage patch. He confessed that he had told the hippo to stay away from such places as cabbage patches. The worst thing that could happen would be the destruction of the animal, which would also result in his own death. Therefore, he contended, that no malice was involved.

According to the court, though, there was malice in the animal's actions. Apparently the defendant had made the mistake of boasting of his crime to the wrong people before the trial.

The defendant was found guilty "because those who have hippopotamuses as their bush souls must know how to control them."

Indeed.

JAPANESE WERE-FOX

Bernhardt J. Hurwood told this story, related by a Japanese student studying in America, in his book *Terror by Night*. The story involved her uncle and his encounter with a supernatural creature in Japan.

The man was returning home from a party, taking with him a package containing food he had not eaten. Being weary, he wanted to get home as quickly as possible. A rice field stretched before him and afforded a nice shortcut.

His pace was steady and grew more rapid with his every step. Alone in the moonlight, his solitude was beginning to take an effect on him. There were terrible *things* lurking in the shadows of night, he knew, and he did not want to encounter any of them.

He had traveled a considerable distance when he heard ominous sounds behind him. Apparently, someone, or something, was following him, wearing silk clothing that rustled in the wind.

Turning, the man saw a beautiful young woman in a fine kimono. He knew that she must have been there all along, but he still could not explain her sudden appearance. He could think of nothing to say.

At last she began to speak, asking if he would give her something to eat. But he was not about to give up his precious food to someone who could so obviously afford to buy her own.

The girl, angered by his refusal to share his food, began to stalk toward him like a prowling animal. As she came nearer, she again asked for food. Once again he refused.

Evidently, the man had gone too far. The girl grabbed the bag of food and prepared to eat what he had taken from the party.

He was not, however, the type to be robbed — especially by a young woman. Immediately, he yanked the parcel of leftovers from her hands.

What then followed made the man wish he had, indeed, let her keep the package.

Instead of again retrieving the food, the woman transformed into a fox! The beast snarled angrily and advanced toward him. No parcel of food was worth an attack by a hungry were-fox. He let the food drop before the animal, then fled into the night, leaving the were-fox to its second-hand meal.

"He soon emerged in the form
of a wolf"

THE WERE-WOLVES·

BIBLIOGRAPHY

Ahmed, Rollo. *The Black Art.* New York: Paperback Library edition, 1968.

Elg, Stefan. *Beyond Belief.* New York: Tower Publications, 1967.

Fielding, William J. *Strange Superstitions.* Doubleday and Company, 1945.

Fodor, Nandor. "Lycanthropy as a Psychic Mechanism." *Journal of American Folklore.* (December 1945), p. 310.

Hill, Douglas, and Pat Williams. "Would You Believe a Werewolf?" *Fate.* Vol. 22-No. 9 (September 1969), 36-43.

Hurwood, Bernhardt J. *The Dark Dominion.* New York: Paperback Library, 1970.

— *Monsters Galore.* New York: Fawcett Publications, 1965.

—*Terror by Night.* New York: Lancer Books, 1963.

—*Vampires, Werewolves, and Ghouls.* New York: Ace Books, 1968.

James, Farley. "The House of the Loup-Garou." *Strange Fate.* Edited by Curtis and Mary Fuller. New York: Paperback Library, 1965.

Jones, G. "Stories of West African Juju." *The Listener.* (August 21,1947).

Keel, John A. *Strange Creatures from Time and Space.* New York: Fawcett Publication, 1970.

Kennerley, Juba. *The Terror of the Leopard Men.* London: S. Paul and Company, 1940.

"Making of a Werewolf, The." *Fate.* Vol. 21-No. 5 (May, 1968), p.48.

Michelet, Jules. *Satanism and Witchcraft.* Translated by A. R. Allinson. New York: the Citadel Press, 1939.

Mills, C. P. "The Were-Tigers of the Assam Hills." *Journal S.P.R.* XX, 1922.

O'Donnell, Elliott. *Werewolves.* London; 1912, and New York: Longvue Press, 1965.

Rawcliffe, D. H. *Illusions and Delusions of the Supernatural and the Occult.* New York: Dover Publications, 1959.

Seabrook, William. *Witchcraft: Its Power in the World Today.* New York: Harcourt, Brace & Company, 1940.

Smith, Warren. *Strange Monsters and Madmen.* New York: Popular Library, 1969.

Spektor, A., Ph.D., personal letters, 1972-1982.

Summers, Montague. *The Werewolf.* London: Routledge and Kegan Paul, and New Hyde Park: University Books, 1966.

—*Witchcraft and Black Magic.* London: Rider and Company, 1946.

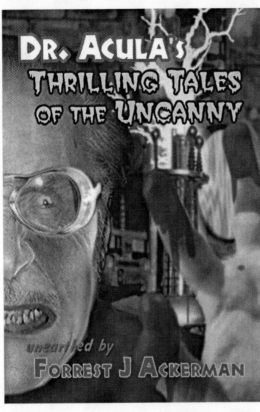

SENSE OF WONDER PRESS
2004 Catalogue

ACKERMANTHOLOGY
Compiled by Forrest J Ackerman
Introduction by John Landis
6x9, 308 pages

Trade Paper	0-918736-25-0	$19.95
Trade Cloth	0-918736-59-5	$34.95

ANARQUÍA
An Alternate History of the Spanish Civil War
by Brad Linaweaver and J. Kent Hastings
Just nominated for "Prometheus Award for Best Novel"
6x9, 237 pages, Illustrated

Trade Paper	0-918736-33-1	$21.95
Trade Cloth	0-918736-50-1	$35.95

CLAIMED
by Francis Stevens
Selected by Forrest J Ackerman
"One of the strangest and most compelling science fantasy novels you will ever read." —H.P. Lovecraft
6x9, 192 pages, Illustrated

Trade Paper	0-918736-37-4	$15.95
Trade Cloth	0-918736-57-9	$27.95

DR. ACULA'S THRILLING TALES OF THE UNCANNY
Compiled by Forrest J Ackerman, 6x9, 265 pages, Illustrated

Trade Paper	0-918736-30-7	$19.95
Trade Cloth	0-918736-61-7	$34.95

Expanded Science Fiction Worlds of
FORREST J ACKERMAN & FRIENDS PLUS
By Forrest J Ackerman with 7 new collaborations
6x9, 205 pages, Illustrated

Trade Paper	0-918736-26-9	$17.95
Trade Cloth	0-918736-58-7	$28.95

FAMOUS FORRY FOTOS
Kodakerman Memories by Forrest J Ackerman
6x9, 117 pages, Photos
Trade Paper	0-918736-32-3	$14.95
Trade Cloth	0-918736-56-0	$34.95

LON OF 1000 FACES!
by Forrest J Ackerman
8.5x11, 300 pages, Illustrations, 1000+ Photos
Trade Paper	0-918736-39-0	$29.95
Trade Cloth	0-918736-53-6	$54.95

THE MAGIC BALL FROM MARS and STARBOY
By Carl L. Biemiller, Introduction by Anne Hardin
6x9, 302 pages, Illustrated, Ages 7-12
Trade Paper	0-918736-09-9	$19.95
Trade Cloth	0-918736-10-2	$38.95

MARTIANTHOLOGY
Compiled by Forrest J Ackerman
Edited by Anne Hardin
6x9, 266 pages, Illustrated
Trade Paper	0-918736-45-5	$19.95
Trade Cloth	0-918736-46-3	$34.95

METROPOLIS
Novel by Thea von Harbou with "Stillustrations" from
Fritz Lang*s film by the same title.
8.5x11, 262 pages, Illustrated
Trade Paper	0-918736-35-8	$23.95
Trade Cloth	0-918736-54-4	$45.95
Ltd. Edition	0-918736-34-X	$60.00

RAINBOW FANTASIA
35 Spectrumatic Tales of Wonder
Selected by Forrest J Ackerman
Introduction by Anne Hardin
6x9, 562 pages, Illustrated
Trade Paper	0-918736-36-6	$29.95
Trade Cloth	0-918736-60-9	$44.95

TRUE VAMPIRES OF HISTORY
by Donald F. Glut
6x9, 132 pages, Illustrated
Trade Paper   0-918736-67-6 $14.95
Trade Cloth   0-918736-68-4 $23.95

TRUE WEREWOLVES OF HISTORY
by Donald F. Glut, Illustrated
6x9, 136 pages, Illustrated
Trade Paper   0-918736-69-2 $14.95
Trade Cloth   0-918736-70-6 $23.95

WOMANTHOLOGY
Compiled & edited by
Forrest J Ackerman and Pam Keesey
6x9, 363 pages, Illustrated
Trade Paper   0-918736-33-1 $21.95
Trade Cloth   0-918736-50-1 $35.95

Complete Story/Author lists for all Ackermanthologies at:

http:\\www.senseofwonderpress.com

Order from all major bookstores including amazon.com,
barnesandnoble.com or directly from Sense of Wonder Press
through our secure shopping cart.

Printed in the United States
148509LV00004B/58/A